CONCEIVABLE

The Unlimited Potential of the Unborn

Pastor Ray Lane

outskirts
press

Conceivable
The Unlimited Potential of the Unborn
All Rights Reserved.
Copyright © 2024 Pastor Ray Lane
v3.0

The opinions expressed in this manuscript are solely the opinions of the author and do not represent the opinions or thoughts of the publisher. The author has represented and warranted full ownership and/or legal right to publish all the materials in this book.

This book may not be reproduced, transmitted, or stored in whole or in part by any means, including graphic, electronic, or mechanical without the express written consent of the publisher except in the case of brief quotations embodied in critical articles and reviews.

Outskirts Press, Inc.
http://www.outskirtspress.com

ISBN: 978-1-9772-6922-5

Cover Photo © 2024 Pastor Ray Lane. All rights reserved - used with permission.

Scripture references from NIV Bible.

Outskirts Press and the "OP" logo are trademarks belonging to Outskirts Press, Inc.

PRINTED IN THE UNITED STATES OF AMERICA

APPRECIATION

To Jamie Belt and the crew at
Outskirts Press for their excellence
and patience in the endeavor.

DEDICATION

This book is dedicated to my siblings and the multiple millions of other aborted babies that never saw the light of day, never smelled a rose, never experienced love, never experienced victory, never experienced defeat, never experienced LIFE on earth. Never had the joy of achieving any contribution to enrich their society.

Table of Contents

Introduction i

1. Potential 1
2. Imaginable (17–21) 14
3. Thinkable (21–38) 22
4. Evident (39–41) 29
    Photo Album 38
5. Possible (41–69) 48
    Conclusion 85
    Addendum 86
    Addendum II 89
    Endorsements 91
    Acknowledgements 94
    Supporting Friends and Family 94

INTRODUCTION

This writing is written to describe the unlimited potential of the unborn.

This is one man's story of his life <u>experiences</u> from before birth through other near-death <u>experiences</u> such as drownings, car wrecks (one on a highway at 80 mph), hearing a bullet go by his head (it sounds like a bumblebee), being gored by a bull (they are bullies), pulling out of a stalled plane at low altitude, and overturned tractors. More than those events, it is about the many ways God has shaped, influenced, protected, and used Ray's life, both in identifiable ways and times that can only be defined as beyond coincidence. Nay sayers will comment that this is only one man's story … that is the idea. The Spirit of our Creator God was/is with him, to teach, guide, and protect. The same is true for any and every situation where we find ourselves. As Billy Graham always said, "The Bible tells us so."

Ray's life can be divided into segments: pre-birth through high school, military and college life, farmer/breeder of registered Holsteins, co-pastor with Norma, police chaplain, assistant funeral director, sheriff's department volunteer, hospice chaplain volunteer, teacher/facilitator, caregiver, writer, and husband of Norma, Jean, Muriel, and Joyce. The first three died of natural deaths … I needed to add that fact.

All this is written simply to let the world know the potential that has been lost every time a baby is aborted. Half the babies aborted might have had significant problems in life, and that thought has been sold as "a bill of goods" to the world. But the other half could have had lives similar to the one in this true story. Then, half the aborted children would also have had above-normal IQs. Do we cry over terminated lives? ... I do.

In 1970 God had called my wife and I to go into Christian ministry as pastors. We sold a very successful farm and dairy herd and moved to Colorado to go to Bible college for training.

We left college to be pastors of six different churches over the years in Los Alamos, New Mexico, Kuna, Idaho, two in Auckland, New Zealand, Spokane, Washington, and before Norma's health led to retirement, Santa Clara, California, in the midst of Silicon Valley. The measure of successful ministry is, "Do you leave the church in better shape than it was when you came?" The world counts numbers; we do some, but seeing people grow in expressing their walk with Him is of first importance ... every other aspect of a local church will be good if the Spirit is in charge.

1

POTENTIAL

In a time long past, there was a beginning. Most Bibles start with that exact wording "in the beginning," but that's a little farther back than I am suggesting. I want to go back and look at your beginning, as a reader of this story. It is your story as well as mine, for we all have had the exact same beginning.

Our beginning started when a specific perfect one or more cells or eggs in your mother's ovary was chosen to be one half the DNA of who you were going to be. The second, or other, half would be a chosen single entity from a stream of tiny, funny-looking, live tadpole-like creatures provided by your father. (Tadpoles are the larval stage in the life cycle of an amphibian—an animal that lives in water and sometimes on land.) When they met, your mom's egg allowed just the right one (or in some cases, one or more babies are conceived; since you don't have a twin brother or sister then, most of the time, only one was selected) to join with the right egg, as it attached itself to the wall of the womb. Actually, I was never a part of Mom's body, and unlike my siblings, in the fullness of time, I would painfully arrive for the life you will be reading about. (If you want a more technical explanation, go to Addendum II for a world-famous Doctors words).

That was our beginning to fulfill God-the-Father's directive, "let us make man (male and female) in our Image: 'We are a Person,' said the Spirit to the Father and Son, so that new person must have the same characteristics as We have."

Therefore, you at the beginning have achieved the first of the three aspects of being like the triune God; you have become a person with a living spirit (that happened when the egg and sperm joined together) that is the immortal part of us. When the egg attached itself to the womb, it began to grow, because it had a life-giving source, to become a human body, and at birth, it became the physical image of the invisible Godhead, plus with your first breath of air, you became a life-force that has a brain, that will have a mind of its own to grow and develop just as your body does.

Therefore, you have fulfilled God-the-Father's directive and are "the image of the triune God." But you must remember that you are an image, limited by a body that is far from perfect ... not quite God. Along with a brain, you were granted "free will," which means that in your mind your choices can agree with what a Holy God thinks and believes or what you as a person think is right.

It is gonna be a "me versus thee" conflict until we finally decide, through our errors, mistakes, and missteps, that He always knows what is best for us, and that our personal thoughts and choices are questionable. That's a flaw that we live with, being born from imperfect people into an imperfect world with an imperfect brain.

God and the life of contributing to American society is to be good for this author who barely escaped being aborted. But in spite of the imperfectness around us, our spiritual control center _can_ be perfect in motive. Jesus said in Matthew 5:8, "Blessed are the pure in heart, for they shall see God." What God says is truth, so it is a fact that we can have a 100% pure heart, not just 99+% as the old soap ad says. Our motives can be pure.

And so you began to develop the physical and spiritual aspects that you are going to need. There is an elementary area developing in the brain from day one that is spiritual in that it concerns right and wrong and it develops for the full life of the person. Going through discovery of accountability, discovery of a relationship with Him, and being His bride spiritually when we say "I DO" with the commitment to say "He is Lord of my life."

The esteemed seventeenth-century French scientist, mathematician, inventor, and philosopher Blaise Pascal said, "There is a God-shaped vacuum in the heart of each man which cannot be satisfied by any man created thing, but only by God the Creator, made known through Jesus Christ." It's hard to understand, but you are going to be a visible image of the God that is unseen.

Somewhere in that grey mush we call brain, there is a segment of mind that will recognize what is moral and immoral, right and wrong. You will have all the qualities that God has, BUT, I say again, you <u>must</u> remember that you are an image, limited by a physical body that is far from perfect … not quite God. You will have free will, which means that in your mind your choices can agree with what a Holy God thinks and believes, or what you as a person think is right. This has led multitudes of individuals to think they are God and the world around them is destined to suffer their self-righteousness.

Now, what's in a name? It gives identity, for you (more on that later) and for God. Where I live is a large retirement community in the midst of thousands of seniors where name recognition is a sometimes thing: "Hi" or "Hey you" will suffice.

When a name is needed for the Creator, "God" usually applies … Yahweh Elohim in the Hebrew with modifiers is always to be respected, honored, obeyed, and worshiped. This

Creator God can never be identified as Allah. Our God has always lived and will never die. You didn't exist until conceived … AND YOUR BODY WILL DIE … your spirit, which can be understood as being in the control center of your soul, will either exist as alive with Yahweh in heaven or be dying ETERNALLY in hell without God … without understanding or actively disliking God. Many seem to have the idea that hell wouldn't be that bad a place.

One of the main features of the person we call God is that we are told by a much-loved friend of God, the apostle John, over and over that "Yahweh is love … God is love."

It can be argued that in a perfect world you first came into being in the mind of two loving individuals that want to be known as Mom and Dad. For the purpose of this narrative, we need to stick to that for a while at least, to the concept that you are a much-desired child in the making.

My friend Betty has a story to tell: "When my son and his wife were expecting their second child, the doctor took some liquid from the embryo to test and told them that there was something wrong with the developing child and recommended an abortion. My son and his wife tossed this decision back and forth for a couple weeks before deciding to keep the baby. Now, 30 years later this young man has a law degree and passed the bar. My grandson is a beautiful, loving person." (Notice the description of what was in the womb.)

Our time of growing in the womb may mean, among many things, that we might have feet with toes for balance, maybe like a young man that goes to university in a Southern state and develops a great throwing arm and abilities directed by his brain and becomes a much-adored All-American football player. There will be a whole lot to say about the brain (the center of everything), but be patient.

POTENTIAL

In his book, Dr. Thomas Verny, gives startling new evidencebased on two decades of medical research.

Your unborn baby is:

- Capable of learning
- Able to warn you of medical problems you and your doctor may not be aware of
- Able to hear and respond to voices and sounds—including music
- Sensitive to his parents' feelings about him
- Capable of responding to love
- An active, feeling human being.

The ways in which you respond to and care for your unborn child may affect his physical and emotional well-being for the rest of his life. The choices you make today about your child's birth may make a vital difference for years to come. You can prepare your unborn baby for a happy, healthy life. This remarkable book will show you how!"

Our developing brain will know how to attract attention for sure in about nine months. Soon it will understand and perhaps resist moral and ethical things like "yes" and "no." Not too long after that the concept of <u>faith</u> comes into action … you believe you can walk because your parents and grandma and grandpa said so … you can fall and get up and eventually walk, then run. It is the possible beginning of faith.

Time flies, and you get to do some twisting and turning and then there is a very painful event. You leave your mother's body because you were never intended to stay there anyway; you were always your own person. Before you knew it, you learned a language, then you briefly learned to say "NO!" And there were more lessons. In the old days it might have meant an application of soap IN the mouth. That experience was transmitted to the spiritual center in the brain and a decision is made—hopefully not to do that again.

AGE 0 MINUS EIGHT MONTHS:

In 1931 in the midst of the Great Depression, a young Idaho wife met with her family doctor and said, "I need another abortion" (Mom said she already had two). His response was: "You are a young farm wife. Your husband is intelligent, inventive, and industrious. With one seven-year-old son, you have fruit, milk, eggs, bacon … why do you want another abortion?" "Well, Dad wants it." "Where is your husband?" "He's out in the car waiting." "Can you go and ask him if he will come in, Doctor Noble* would like to talk with him." (*Name changed). She did and he came in and talked with the doctor so the baby that could have died … LIVED.

> *In the book WHAT EVER HAPPENED TO THE HUMANRACE? written by Francis Schaeffer in 1979. Dr. C. Everett Koop, Surgeon General under President Reagan, says: "killing a human being any time after the day of conception is murder."

Many abortions (they were illegal then, but the law was not uniformly enforced) happened, but one baby born in 1932 was me … Raymond Dee Lane.

The house on the farm was a two-story affair with two unheated bedrooms upstairs and a kitchen and living room downstairs. A wood-fired stove in the kitchen and a wood/coal-fired heater in the living room provided all the heat for the entire house. Water was pumped by hand from the well just outside the back door. Water then arrived in the house by bucket or pitcher. The cellar was a covered pit dug in the backyard that stored canned goods and was big enough to walk in. There was an ice box in the house that worked with deliveries of blocks of ice. The outhouse was, of course, a small two-hole facility near the house. The farm buildings consisted of the house, a garage for the Model A Ford, a henhouse, a milking barn, and a shed. The buildings had been built on an 80-acre land-grant farm that had been cleared of sagebrush about 1900 when irrigation water came into new canals throughout the Boise Valley—now Treasure Valley.

Who could have imagined that a boy born into a struggling Idaho farm family would ever have joined as an adult with his wife (more about her later) in having a leisurely breakfast in Washington State with Bill and Gloria Gaither, perhaps the best known and respected Christian music personalities in the world.

Who could have imagined that this man would often personally join in Colorado with Dr. James Dobson in hands-on prayer. Jim is the founder of Focus on the Family, an organization with awesome positive Christian influence around the world and whose wife Shirley would visit my ailing wife at our home. Jim's father was the university professor of art that had such a positive effect on our son.

Who could have imagined that this man would be put in the position of giving aid in California to a young man that had gotten into bad company, been shot by gang members for suspected theft from one of them. They had taken him into the hills above San Jose, shot him, and thrown him down an embankment and left him for dead. But he had survived, and when he came into my life seeking help he still had eight .22-caliber slugs scattered throughout his body. Help was provided ... More later.

Before I went to school, I was adept at picking cherries, apples, and apricots. I could plant and harvest a garden. I could put the bridle on a horse (even a mean one that the only other person who could do it was Dad), ride a horse, and drive a team. Looking back, it seems to me that God had put some special quality in me that enabled me to work with animals. (God gives everyone a talent of some kind.) I could crawl under the mean horse or the electric fence and bring the cows in from pasture. One year there was a parade in Boise that, among other things, had a competition to see who had the ugliest dog. That was the first ribbon that came my way. Don't laugh ... it was earned!

I also knew where roast beef came from. Dad butchered a steer on the farm and I helped cut up the meat. Some people think it just comes from a store. Chicken to fry came from the chopping block in the backyard. Part of my respect for **life** happened on the farm. It really hurt when I raised a lamb and he became lamb chops. We didn't get our milk from a store either. We had to work for it.

Then, there were pigs. I knew it took a boar and a sow to create piglets and that when the sow was giving birth, there needed to be a railing about six inches from the floor of the birthing stall for the babies to get under so that the mother didn't accidentally lie on them. Think about it ... we try to save baby pigs and think that aborting human babies is okay. Please try to remember that this book is all about what it has meant to learn and <u>experience</u>. In other words, our learning starts long before school and continues long after.

Once upon a time, there was a scientist named Darwin. He came up with a theory of evolution for the development of mankind. This theory could never be proven, because it was never true. Evolution joined the trash heap of history, joining the flat earth society and the sun circles the earth theory—both of which apparently had elites that would kill you if you disagreed with them. Knowledge of DNA, developed in the middle of the 20th century, sealed the doom of Darwinian evolution. It is harder now to get rid of the idea that a baby isn't a baby until some time picked out of the air … two months … heartbeat … six months—just whatever some elite government person says. These elites don't physically kill anyone, they just censor and call names and say you aren't Woke.

School was wonderful. When my daughter arrived she was named after my first-grade teacher, Leah Peterson. I was and am curious about almost everything, and that is basic to learning. She and her husband would later go on to Alaska, where the salary was high to entice teachers to come into the wilderness. He became the State Superintendent of Public Education, and she taught and wrote many textbooks. I visited Dr. Leah in her penthouse in Peterson Tower in downtown Anchorage when she was in her late 90s. Wonderful philanthropist. It seems that soon after they had arrived in Alaska during WWII that their jobs paid well, and because of the fact that Leah had grown up on a ranch in the hills of central Idaho and was very frugal, they would buy a piece of land in a village called Anchorage. They bought and sold. Then they had bought and sold some more … again and again … in boomtown.

My transportation to and from school was by riding my bicycle the mile and a quarter on the side of two-lane US 30 (now four-lane Fairview), the old Oregon Trail road.

There was a prune orchard along the road, and I still love fresh prunes in the fall. When added up, that came to about a thousand miles … and no, it wasn't uphill both ways, nor was the snow knee-deep. It was level and only a few really inclement weather days.

I can't remember a time of not liking any subject in grade school, but geography was a favorite. My love for maps started there with learning all state capitals and capital cities all over the world. I was valedictorian when I finished grade school—another award for the baby that might not have been. Okay, being first among 12 students in a country school may not have been a big deal, but at that time a test was given to all eighth-graders in the county, and that includes the thousands of kids in Ada, the most populous county in Idaho. For several weeks after taking the test, I arrived at school early to find out how I scored because I knew it went well. The morning that the scores were in, Mrs. Anthony was frowning as she handed me the scores. She said I should have done better. I had missed three questions. One because I misread the question. For one I knew the answer but apparently in a hurry checked the wrong answer. One, I just flat-out didn't know the answer. Anyway, third in the county wasn't too bad. I think about my early schooling and compare it in a way with my one grandson that took an SAT test after high school, and when 1,600 was a perfect score, that is what he received. He also attended Colorado School of Mines, and when he graduated in 2015 he received a special award for Top Computer Engineer. He is now working for a firm that is on the ground with AI looking for cures for cancer. That is the grandson (of course others were involved) of the baby that was nearly aborted.

One summer when I was perhaps seven, my brother, who was seven years older, my teenaged aunt, and I went swimming in a canal near Grandpa's farm and tragedy nearly happened for me. I was totally unfamiliar with being in water; I was happily splashing water on the others and stepped into fast-flowing deep water and immediately went under. In the moments before my brother and aunt were able to rescue me, it seemed like I had inhaled and swallowed gallons of water. One step further and I would have been a "goner." God, maybe angels, were watching over me again.

My first job came when I was seven. Dad paid me a nickel a day at harvest time to carry water to the harvest crews. That meant carrying one-gallon glass jugs, wrapped in wet burlap to keep the water cool, to wherever they were needed. Then it became my job at ten or so to drive a team of horses when stacking hay. When I was twelve, I got my first paying job away from home delivering the Sunday newspaper. That meant that my route covered 12 miles back and forth around the sections around home. There were 52 customers out of the 60 homes to receive papers and once a month I would go t to collect for the papers. On collection days I would stop at the few homes that were not taking the paper and would often convince someone to become a new customer. I realized years later that knocking on those doors was good preparation to go door to door as a pastor. I wouldn't do that in urban areas today, but would do it in farm areas.

If three- or ten-speed bikes existed, I'd never heard about it. A few of the miles were gravel and hadn't been paved yet. On occasion, Mom would drive me around the route during a storm or when the side roads were too muddy.

At that time, the only outdoor sport we had in grade school was baseball, which I loved. We played "work-up" at noon and recess. When we traveled to another small school for a game, I was our pitcher. By that time, my brother had been drafted into the Army, so the only way I had to practice at home was to have a rubber ball the size of a tennis ball and throw it against the concrete front step of the house. That way I became accurate as a pitcher and learned to pick up ground balls. Monthly PTA (Parent-Teacher Meetings) were held in the school basement and were great times of showing off student talents. Today, it is my understanding that parent involvement with teachers seems to be frowned upon. Dad was chairman of the school board when a new building was erected.

By the time I was in high school my family had taken a few vacations, which started when our car was a Model A Ford and blossomed to a new 1936 Plymouth. Vacations would start on my birthday, July 6th. and end on Mom's birthday, July 18. I remember going to Yellowstone National Park, seeing bears up close when there were "bear jams" as many cars stopped at the same place and occasionally had a bear in the car when someone disobeyed the sign and tried to feed the bears. We saw Old Faithful, buffalo, and elk.

Other vacations took us to visit relatives in coastal cities and a visit to Catalina Island and a ride on a glass-bottom boat that stimulated my interest in many different fish. A visit to the Oregon coast to see Mom's uncle meant we got to pick up agates and sea shells at Agate Beach, see the sea lions, and the Astoria Lighthouse. Another time the main attraction was the 1939 Golden Gate International Exposition on Treasure Island in San Francisco Bay. For many years we also went camping and fishing in the mountains of Idaho. I didn't realize until much later that I could have missed all that like my aborted siblings did.

High school meant four letters in baseball; the first came because I played a few innings behind our star pitcher Vernon Law, who would receive the Cy Young Award for being the most effective National League pitcher with the Pittsburgh Pirates in 1960. I was the athlete in the family, while my brother had played a trumpet in the band before me.

POTENTIAL

In my early years, I seemed to have a built-in awareness of good and bad. In my freshman year, the school was like a facility where the inmates ran the asylum. I got embarrassed once in a terrible way. The juniors and seniors made life miserable for the younger students, and it was allowed by the administration. A couple of school organizations extended an invitation to join, but then I heard about the informal initiations such as walking a gauntlet between lines of older members, being swatted hard with a wooden paddle, and having eggs broken on your head as some of the lesser hazings. I said "no thanks."

The next year a new administration came in, and when some of us visited with the superintendent, he put a stop to all the demeaning activities that were happening. Later, when I did join a club, the boys that had taken the punishment the year before weren't too happy that they didn't get to take revenge on incoming members.

More about classes later.

2
IMAGINABLE (17–21)

After high school I started college (the first ever in my family). But the Korean War was on and I had a low draft number, so my buddy Don Jasica and I decided to join the 190th Idaho Air National Guard on 1-3-1951 to avoid the draft. On 1-10-51 the unit was drafted along with units from North Dakota, Montana, and Los Angeles to form a "wing".

We served 21 months active duty that was kind of like a farm boy getting an education of barracks social life. There was a card game to enjoy called 52 Pickup (ask someone) … okay, I found out it meant a "friend" would throw a deck of cards in the air, and you are to pick them up. I learned to play chess fairly well, and a multitude of other games. Like college it was a time of sex education. Sex on the farm was different from what city kids learned.

I learned to march and enjoyed that. My duties were the mostly mundane marking of cards to keep track of every nut, bolt, truck, tire, and every part for P-51s. The last part of active duty, I was assigned to the ammo dump and handled multitudes of metal boxes of .50-calibre bullets. Also mixing napalm … stuff that looked like sawdust with gasoline for practice bombs at the time. (I had to quit smoking for a while.) When we went on active duty during the Korean War, our squadron had to upgrade from F-51s to F-86 jets, so that took our whole active-duty time so we never saw combat.

The first part of our active time was spent at Moody Air Force Base, near Valdosta, Georgia. My life prior to that time had all been in the arid West. That base was near Okefenokee Swamp and humidity was totally new to me. The only way to get even remotely cool was with swamp coolers and fans. Refrigerated cooling had not arrived there yet. We were always wet before our shower in the morning. I couldn't believe people actually lived there.

Pneumonia did come my way, bad enough that I was in the base hospital. It was there that I experienced what is referred to as "death and dying." In the middle of the night, the struggle to breathe stopped and a dark hallway opened before me to walk toward a bright light ... it was quiet and very peaceful. Like multitudes of others, I can only conclude God had further plans for me.

It seems like the biggest events of my life during the active duty time did not relate to military life. Following the time in Georgia, we were moved to Victorville, California, in the Mojave Desert. I loved it. In part, it was because we were only 830 miles from home, meaning that we could get a one-day pass for Friday and a group of us would get together and leave the base at 5 p.m. Thursday with three drivers and arrive home between 5 and 6 the next morning. (There was no speed limit in Nevada.) I would sleep an hour, have breakfast with my folks, and chase girls until Sunday 5 o'clock and make the return trip. We could make roll call, take a nap, and all was well.

On one of those trips, as we were traveling at least 80 mph through Nevada, the car lights revealed a herd of horses that suddenly appeared along both sides of the road where they were grazing. Somehow we missed all of them because not one was crossing the road as we sped by. Nevada had open range at the time, and we were familiar with stories of how people who were cleaning up wrecks could tell how fast a car had been traveling when it hit a cow or horse. If you were going fast enough, a cow would go clear over the car. Lesser speeds meant that the critter would come through the windshield.

One more near tragedy while in the service. One of my best friends had his Baptist brother come to visit and we went to see the Pacific Ocean for fun. At Santa Monica Beach, it was essentially required that we go in the water. I could "dog paddle" a little, and the brothers could swim just a little. There was an area close to shore where splashing around was safe for me. But the brothers discovered that beyond a brief area of deep, there was a significant area of shallow water where we could splash in the waves. So I got out to join them, and when it was time to get on dry land I tried to get back in, but the waves kept knocking me back into the deep. One brother worked to get me in until he was exhausted, then the other tried, and all the time I was getting waterlogged. Finally I was able to get a toehold in the sand and make it out. All three of us collapsed on the beach for a while. That was the lifetime end of swimming for me. But there would be even more times when God seems to have intervened for me. Aah, experiences, experiences.

Soon there was more college. This was where my interest in all things political seemed to come together, so a brief interlude.

It happens fairly often that someone wants to know what sources I use for my political thinking. It might help when putting that information together if my background could be considered. I have shared this information many times, but finally it is going to be something that is on file to be found and shared. In part it is difficult because some might think of it as bragging. It is not, it is fact. The apostle Paul is my mentor in this. In II Corinthians 11 & 12, besides being a student of the great teacher Gamaliel, he describes experiences as to why he is worth listening to. Many have listened to him and many have not.

When President Franklin D. Roosevelt was on some of his "barnstorming" cross-country tours, my parents took me as an 8- or 9-year-old to hear him speak from the back of the caboose on the presidential train in Boise, Idaho. Dad didn't much care for FDR but he was president ... it was dramatic even though he hid the fact that he was in a wheelchair. It was a few years later that I found out that little bit of deception that led to the shaping of my attitude about politicians.

Dad always tried to keep informed in the political arena. At one time he was State Grange Master, a position in which politicians would call to ask his opinion about how farmers were doing. Later he would be president of the Agrarian Club, an organization of 100+ in Ada County, the home of the state capital. It was an organization where you had to be invited to join, made up of respected farmers, business owners like implement dealers such as John Deere and Massey Harris, animal food dealers like Purina, leading cattlemen, dairymen, sheep herders, and chicken and hog farmers; there were specialists in each of those categories. Then there were the politicians, county agents, county commissioners, and sometimes state representatives keeping us informed as to what was going on in the legislature. It was a club to spread information about what was happening in the agricultural world and did have some political influence. A few years later I was president of that club as well. I began the practice of saying grace before the meals (a practice that if the club still exists may still be in effect). Three other agricultural organizations with a small bit of political connection, including the Idaho State Holstein Club, would call me president. It seems rather interesting to me that the baby Dad didn't want would follow in his "foot tracks." My older brother was State President of the Idaho Rural Mail Carriers and a Chief Master Sergeant through his 32 years in Army Reserves in Army Intelligence. I wonder what our siblings might have done.

Backing up a number of years for political interest, one of the most interesting classes that came my way was Idaho government in grade school. In high school there was a class on American government that led to memorizing some great speeches and documents. That class resulted in a copy of the Constitution always being close at hand.

About 2005 I took an online course by the title Constitution 101 from Hillsdale College. An awesome course that introduced me to Wall Builders, an organization focusing on American history with an emphasis on the moral and religious applications of our Constitution. In 2008 or 2010 I was elected to be a delegate from my precinct to Colorado's El Paso County Republican Caucus. In 2022 I represented my precinct in the Douglas County Caucus in Colorado. That county is about the size of the state of Delaware.

After the short tour of duty with the Air Force, a night "speech" class in our community college opened up an interesting situation. There "happened" to be two long classes with a break between them. The teachers were two young lawyer friends, and during break those two invited me as an older person just out of the military to join them in brief discussions. One was Frank Church, who would soon become U.S. Senator (D) from Idaho and had a distinguished twenty-year career there, and was a serious Democratic Party candidate for President in 1976. Some of what he set up for hearings was vital for setting up U.S. congregational hearings in 2023. Have I mentioned lately that I have had a lot of interesting experiences?

In the 2000 retirement in Colorado Springs, there was an invitation to join a Bible study class at the home of Kent Lambert (R), majority leader at the time of the Colorado State Assembly. He would almost always rush in late and tell us what had gone on that day, so a dozen or so of us knew what was going on before the papers came out in the morning. Kent was always respected across the aisle. He is a retired Air Force Academy colonel and I joined him on the fifty-yard line for the AF-Army football game. (Can you imagine?) Also during that time of retirement in Colorado Springs during the Tea Party, U.S. Representative from Colorado Doug Lamborn, currently a member of the U.S. House Armed Services Committee and chairman of the Strategic Forces Subcommittee, became an acquaintance (distant). I had frequent conversations with his Colorado field man whom I had met in the Bear Cafe in Woodland Park. I have been in touch with Lamborn's office this year.

Kevin Kiley was the minority leader in the CA assembly. Another Christian, he was recommended to me about five years ago by a stepdaughter and layman from the church where I was pastor in Santa Clara. Kevin was a high school teacher and is an attorney and very active foe of Governor Newsom. He is part of the new crew of Republicans in D.C. House. He can be seen frequently on interviews for TV. He has become known as so good with his questioning of people, giving testimony before at least two main committees in which other representatives frequently give their time to him. My name is on the list for letters that he sends out frequently that usually contain some places to get a lot of video of what is happening that he is directly involved in, as well as more general observations. Awesome!

Calvin Johnson, retired AF Major, navigator on all the

biggest aircraft, major contributions to creating the cockpit of the B-1 Stealth Bomber. Currently civilian contractor at Schriever AFB in Colorado Springs ... a top-secret activity. He has two majors from the University of Idaho—one in physics and the other in political science. At one time, as a teenager, he worked for me on the farm. When my son died six years ago, I asked him if he would take Jeff's place in my life. We meet from time to time and he sends non-secret information to me weekly.

Those individuals and sources have given me information that has shaped my life. If you haven't figured it out by now I'm conservative. So were/are all my wives and 9 of 10 stepchildren. Thirty-eight of the 40 volunteers I served with were also conservative. The only reason the other two could give was that their parents were of a different bent.

The college I was attending was Boise Junior College (Now Boise State University). Boise has always been crazy about football, and in the fall of 1950 they went to the Junior Rose Bowl (me, the unwanted, in the good seats) in Pasadena to play Tyler, Texas. The next year they went to the Potato Bowl in California. A group of us went to both games ... cheering "HIT THEM ... HIT THEM AGAIN ... HARDER ... HARDER." The second bowl game happened because by then I was in the Air Force and stationed in Victorville, CA. <u>You haven't lived</u> if you have never been to a football bowl game.

Oh yes, there were classes at college too. I took a psychology class first term that led me to believe that I knew everything, while knowing very little. Others may have found good use of that field. My favorite courses were in the sciences. One class with special memories was engineering chemistry for which I had no background. The first day of class there were about 120 students in a room that would seat about 80. The professor, Dr. Obe, announced that the class was so difficult that only perhaps as many as 20 would get a passing grade. The next day there were about 60 present. I stayed and studied hard and was getting all A's until one Friday I skipped class to go deer hunting on the opening day of hunting that I had never missed. On Monday the prof had a pop quiz on what we had learned on Friday. I received an F on that. I ended up with a B+ as a final grade instead of an A because of that. About 15 others passed the class.

It was on one of my many deer-hunting trips that I was stalking for deer through the brush and I heard a *buzz-bang*. A hunter on a hillside across the gully had apparently shot toward movement in the brush. The bullet must have passed within inches of my ear. I had scope on my 270, so I took a look at him and contemplated notching his ear, but simply let out a shout and he took off in a hurry. (I had a medal for marksmanship from my military time.)

3
THINKABLE (21–38)

I was still only twenty-one when I finished my military duty, so I was living at home doing a lot of chores and milking the dozen cows or so that were on the farm, doing extra work at harvest time that was putting a little money in the bank, while attending college and chasing young ladies several nights a week. There was a year when for some reason I kept count and there were seventeen nice ladies … and no, while there was necking, there was no further sexual activity. Mom had followed a biblical admonition of Paul in writing to Titus in Titus 2:6: "Similarly, encourage young men to be self-controlled." She taught me to respect women and besides, I wanted to marry a virgin, which I did. If any of the young ladies I dated were not virgins when they got married, it wasn't my fault. I have often thought sadly about my aborted siblings and the fact that they missed out on the highs and lows of the courting process. In that seventeen was a Miss Boise and contestant in the state beauty pageant. There was the very shy daughter of a Native American ("Indian" at the time), and an incredibly beautiful daughter of an Armenian family.

Looking back, I cannot explain exactly what I was looking for in a wife, but while beauty was nice, personality was apparently number one. I knew that a man who was planning on being a farmer had a liability to overcome. But it was a search that my three buddies and I entered into with gusto to see who would be married first. We had a hamburger bet on who would win ... big spenders. While we would all have an occasional drink, that wasn't a big part of our lives. One evening one of my buddies, "Buzz" Harold Wehrman, and I came out of a movie at the old Penny Theater in Boise at the same time as a couple of girls. I knew one of them, but her friend, an attractive redhead, caught my eye. We chatted, and no, they were not interested in us taking them home, but the one I knew gave me the phone number of her friend. That may have broken up their friendship, but every couple of days that number was called, and each conversation got a little longer until she finally said she would go with me to a movie. I picked Norma up at the home where she was working for the summer after high school as nanny/housekeeper. The name of the movie has long since been forgotten, but after the movie, we went to a drive-in and had a hot chocolate and talked and talked. She about pushed the passenger door off the whole evening and I don't remember even touching her hand. The next morning I called all my buddies and said, "I HAVE FOUND HER." That was in August, engagement was November college football homecoming. She got a big mum (flower) and a diamond, and we were married in March. After the honeymoon, we came home and two days later took over the farm. I would later agree to buy it on time with Dad holding the mortgage. Even though they had planned to have me aborted, I was treated well.

In a few years awards began to come my way. Twice Kraft Foods Dairyman of the Year for the state of Idaho. Twice Young Farmer of the Year for our county by Junior Chamber of Commerce. Second place State Young Farmer of the Year once. All of these things meant that the county agricultural agent chose my farm operation as a display farm to invite other farmers to come and see how it could be done. Becoming a farmer meant that becoming a mechanic was not an option. Very few new machines arrived on my farm. (When there was a sale before I left the farm, I overheard someone say, "all this machinery is junk" … true.) While the field equipment had seen its day, the means to do a top-notch job with cows was pretty good. It was a time in the '50–'60s of great technological advance in crops and farming in general. One way of bettering myself was to join Toastmasters where we learned how to be better speakers, but spent a lot of time asking each other the question, "Why don't you run for county commissioner? The ones we have are terrible."

I was elected to be president of the Boise Valley DHIA (Dairy Herd Improvement Association), which meant that I was able to lead the way into computer record keeping of dairy cow production records at Washington State University. This helped every milk producer have a finer operation and improve their standard of living.

In the process of time, a herd of registered Holsteins was developed starting with one that had been my FFA (Future Farmers of America) project in high school. That cow and many others won many ribbons in the show ring, including a bull that I developed with another man that was Grand Champion at the Cow Palace in San Francisco and Reserve All-American in 1965. There were perhaps 40 young bulls sold to other farmers in the valley, always a bull from one of my best cows.

I should explain that there is a difference between a dairyman who has a herd of milk cows for the sale of milk for all sorts of purposes and a breeder—a dairy operation where the owner not only plans to sell milk, but has an ability to develop a herd of cows that produce the bulls that are used today through artificial insemination to improve in generation after generation the qualities that create more productive cows. It takes an incredible amount of study to be able to do it well. My choice of breed was Holsteins, because I like big cows producing high volumes of milk.

A dairyman or woman who aims high will almost always be involved in showing members of the herd at shows like state fairs. I've mentioned some of my show ring results that were pretty good. But "the proof is in the pudding." Do they perform?

The last two years of my operation of the dairy, it was the top for pounds per cow in the state … as well as a couple of individual records. The reason this has any significance is that when the herd was sold in 1970, the young heifers went to an outstanding breeder by the name of Andy Hurtgen in California, and his wife told me a couple of years ago that a grandson of one of those cows was sold into artificial service in Canada. That bull's offspring are recorded as the fifth highest production of any bull in national history. The baby that barely got to live played a part in enriching the economy of Canada.

When my operation was sold, the milk cows went one way and the young females—heifers—went in several directions, but in a few years the 44 heifers produced 4 cows that classified excellent for type (looks). That was a phenomenal achievement compared to an average golfer getting a hole in one every ten times he played. Actually breeding that high a percent of excellent would likely get me rated pretty well in animal husbandry. According to the Holstein Association of America, over 300 animals carried my "Adaray" prefix on their names.

Back to showing cattle. It basically meant that a small segment of time the entire year was involved with training some individuals that might have what it took to acquire a blue or purple ribbon.

Ah, the shows, often at state fairs that included carnivals, maybe rodeos, and multiple venues. It meant hauling, washing, clipping, and providing some special feed. Most of the time it required a special someone to stay and care for the animals. My special guy more often than not was Art Johnson. He was a neighbor lad that was my "hired hand." He could do everything that needed doing on the farm. At the fair, part of the fun was listening to what people had to say. The dairymen were always interested in how well a cow's udder was constructed, and did they have good legs and feet for longevity. City people seemed to always admire the bulls. The years on the farm were good for us. One piece of life that began there was that I would write "Letters to the Editor" frequently. Over the years there have likely been at least a hundred "missives" of "good job," "well done," and about equal numbers of "you have to be kidding," usually about some activity that is unethical or just plain foolish. I lost one friend that way and received lots of "YES!!"s.

But there were a few bad things that happened too ... usually because I did something dumb. One time a friend came to visit and see a bull that had recently won a blue ribbon. I got hold of his nose ring and got into the pen to lead the animal around like he was in the show ring. The only difference was that when showing the bull I used a four-foot-long staff to lead the bull. But that day, by just taking hold of the nose ring, I got in the pen to show him off but had no leverage, and the bull soon had me down on the ground and we were literally eye to eye. Fortunately my friend, a couple feet away on the other side of the fence, made enough noise to distract the bull and I scampered out of the pen. Several times I was careless around machinery and could have died in tragic ways. I did have two neighbors that died in gruesome tractor accidents. Several times I have asked God why, or made the statement "only God knows," and one time I clearly heard Him reply to that last statement, "You got that right."

FAMILY

Norma became my wife and we had 57 wonderful years together before she died on her 76th birthday from heart problems. On the farm, we had an occasional traveling salesman come to the door. One was selling the World Book Encyclopedia and I was convinced that our kids would benefit from having a set in the home, so we began monthly payments. Our daughter had very little regard for books throughout regular school years, but later in life she earned her bachelor's degree. The rest of us used them a lot.

About five years into our marriage Norma read an advertisement about Norman Rockwell's correspondence art course; she sent for information telling how it worked and she was hooked. She begged me to pay the $25 a month for three years. Now being a young farmer trying to make ends meet and having little interest or regard for artwork, it took a lot of persuasion for me to think it would be money well spent. I knew that she had received a $100 art scholarship to go to college, but throwing paint at a canvas and calling it art was a waste of time. Anyway I finally gave in by rationalizing that when she got old, she would have something to sit around and do in retirement—stupid, stupid me. Before she had finished the course, she was selling paintings and would be a major support of our ministry life and paint and sell over 1,700 original paintings, including one of the Madonna and child (Mary and Jesus) that is priceless and hangs in the livingroom today. Also to grace the photo album as a frameable 5X7 for art lovers.

We had two children: a daughter that is an outstanding

massage therapist in Texas and a son that among other occupations involving his MA in medical illustration, taught school in the Vanguard charter school in Colorado Springs. He helped that school become the top-ranked in their category in the state. He had a son, my one grandchild. He now works from home in Montana for a London firm while finishing his PhD having to do with the atoms in segment 19 of the DNA ... an area working toward a cure for cancer. That is the grandson of a baby that almost never happened.

The murder of babies is one of the most horrible things man can do as far as God is concerned. In the Old Testament He took his time, but eventually both the north and south of ancient Israel paid a terrible price in part because of the treatment of children, and His judgement will be true.

4

EVIDENT (39–41)

In 1962 a neighbor asked if she could take our two young children to a vacation Bible school at her church. I was reluctant again because my few contacts with church had left me with the idea that church was only interested in getting people's money. But I had known this lady all my life (Bernice, the mother of Art, my terrific hired helper, and Calvin, my replacement son), and I knew she was a good person, so I said okay. Besides, free baby sitting was a plus.

The kids came home happy at the end, and Bernice wanted to take them to Sunday school and I said no ... a little bit of religion was probably good, but let's not get carried away.

The next summer it was the same story and same result, only that time I couldn't resist the kids begging to go. After a couple of months, I became alarmed enough to tell Norma, "You better go find out what is going on there."

She went and I had private time so I could do more pheasant hunting or quick fishing trips, though I never planted or harvested on the Lord's Day. Then one Sunday she came home from church and announced, "I got saved today!!!" I said, "Saved—saved from what?"

She couldn't explain it very well, but I quickly noticed that this beautiful redhead seemed to have lost her volatile temper.

I'd grown up with a lot of arguing in the house, so some seemed normal. So, for the next two and a half years she spent her time being gone with the kids on Sunday, introducing me to some outstanding people, and loving me more than ever ... I'm pretty slow, but something good was happening.

Then, one morning two years later, I came in the house and she asked me, "Do you believe in Jesus as Lord?" My reply was approximately "yes, I guess so," and went about my work. Later in the day she said, "God has told me that by making that statement that Jesus was your Lord, you have become a 'born again' Christian." People will say that is not quite how it happens ... well it did for me. In the past couple of years multiple contacts with her church friends convinced me that the idea was good. Anyway, she said the church had been praying for me and asked if she could tell them. I said, "Okay, you can beat a drum, blow a trumpet, or whatever you want." You have to understand that I am pretty low-key.

I wasn't aware of any emotion, but I noticed that the next morning I threw my cigarettes away, got a new language (I quit swearing), and the rare drink of an alcoholic beverage was gone. Though I had never abused family or livestock, everything including the dog seemed to like me better. The next Sunday I went to church for the first time with family, and when the offering plate was passed, I put a check in. THAT was the moment I understood something had happened. I began attending Sunday school and quickly understood that I had been a sinner. My worst sin was that years had been spent without Jesus as Lord. From that point on, I joined Norma in traveling with Jesus and grew rapidly in what is called being "born again." I discovered a whole new and even better way of life. At an annual church election, I ended up as chairman of the board as we went through a building program. Then, I was invited to serve on the board of a good-sized Christian school. Boy, do Christian school administrators get an education. My involvement and spiritual growth was dramatic with multiplying responsibilities in teaching and church administration.

A SIDEBAR NOW

After I had been a Christian a few years, I came across the following item and kept it in a file, only to discover it recently and realize that it has had a massive impact on my approach to life. I don't know where it came from, but perhaps it will strike a note for you as well.

What is the True Meaning of Life?
How can purpose, fulfillment, and satisfaction in life be found?How can something of lasting significance be achieved?

Many people have never stopped to consider these important questions. They look back years later and wonder why their relationships have fallen apart and why they feel so empty, even though they may have achieved what they set out to accomplish. An athlete who had reached the pinnacle of his sport was once asked what he wished someone would have told him when he first started playing his sport. He replied, *"I wish that someone would have told me that when you reach the top, there's nothing there."* Many goals reveal their emptiness only after years have been wasted in their pursuit.

In our humanistic culture, people lose sight of the meaning of life. They pursue many things, thinking that in them they will find meaning and purpose. Some of these pursuits include business success, wealth, good relationships, sex, entertainment, and doing good to others. *People have testified that, while they achieved their goals of wealth, relationship, and pleasure, there was still a deep <u>void inside</u>, a feeling of <u>emptiness</u> that nothing seemed to fill.*

The author of the book of Ecclesiastes looked for the meaning of life in many vain presets. He describes the feeling of emptiness he felt: *"Meaningless! Meaningless!... Utterly meaningless! Everything is meaningless" (Ecclesiastes 1:2).* King Solomon, the writer of Ecclesiastes, had wealth beyond measure, wisdom beyond any man of his time or ours, hundreds of women, palaces and gardens that were the envy of kingdoms, the best food and wine, and every form of entertainment available. He said at one point that anything his heart wanted, he pursued (Eccl. 2:10). And yet he summed up life "under the sun"—life lived as though all there is to life is what we can see with our eyes and experience with our senses—is <u>*meaningless*</u>.

What explains the void? God created us for something beyond what we can experience in the here and now. Solomon said of God, "He has also set eternity in the hearts of men" (Eccl. 3:11).

In our <u>hearts</u> we are aware that the "here-and-now" is not all that there is!

In the book of Genesis, we find a clue to the meaning of life in the fact that God created mankind in His image (Genesis 1:26). *This means that we are <u>more</u> like God than we are like anything else.* We also find that, before mankind fell and the curse of sin came upon the earth, the following things were true:

1. God made man a social creature (Genesis 2:18–25)
2. God gave man work (Genesis 2:15)
3. God had fellowship with man (Genesis 3:8)
4. God gave man dominion over the earth (Genesis 1:26)

These facts have significance related to the meaning of life. God intended mankind to have fulfillment in life, but our condition (especially touching our fellowship with God) was adversely affected by the fall into sin and the resulting curse upon the earth (Genesis 3).

The book of Revelation shows that God is concerned with restoring the meaning of life to us. God reveals that He will destroy his present creation and create a new heaven and a new earth. At that time, He will restore full fellowship with redeemed mankind, while the unredeemed will have been judged unworthy and cast into the lake of fire (Rev. 20:11–15).

The curse of sin will be done away with; there will be no more sin, sorrow, sickness, death, or pain (Rev. 21:4). God will dwell with mankind, and they shall be His children (Rev. 21:7).

Thus, we come full circle: God created us to have fellowship with Him; man sinned, breaking that fellowship; God restores that fellowship fully in the eternal state. To go through life achieving everything we set out to achieve only to die separated from God for eternity would be worse than futile! *But God has made a way to not only make <u>eternal bliss possible</u> (Luke 23:43) but also life on earth <u>satisfying</u> and <u>meaningful!</u>*

How is this eternal bliss and "heaven on earth" obtained?

The Meaning of Life is Restored Through Jesus Christ

The real meaning of life, both now and in eternity, is found in the restoration of our relationship with God. This restoration is only possible through God's Son, Jesus Christ, who reconciles us to God (Romans 5:10; Acts 4:12; John 1:12; 14:6).

<u>Salvation</u> and eternal life are gained when we <u>trust</u> in Jesus Christ as Savior.

Once that salvation is received by grace through faith, Christ makes us new creations, and we begin the progressive journey of growing closer to Him and learning to rely on Him.

God wants us to know the meaning of life. *Jesus said, "I have come that they may have <u>life</u> and have it to the <u>full</u>" (John 10:10).* A "full" life is logically one that is meaningful and devoid of aimless wandering.

The meaning of life is wrapped up in the glory of God. God says, "But now thus saith the Lord that created thee, O Jacob, and he that formed thee, O Israel, Fear not: for I have redeemed thee. I have called thee by <u>name</u>; thou art mine." (Isaiah 43:1) *The reason we were made is for God's glory.* Any time we substitute our own glory for God's, we miss the meaning of life. "If anyone would come after me, he must deny himself and take up his cross and follow me. For whoever wants to save his life will lose it, but whoever loses his life for me will find it" (Matthew 16:24–25).

Delight yourself in the LORD and he will give you the desires of your heart" (Psalm 37:4).

Part of what I gathered from that is that you haven't really lived unless you have been "born again" spiritually. John 3:7 in the Amplified Bible reads: "Do not be surprised that I have told you, 'You must be born again [reborn from above—spiritually transformed, renewed, sanctified].'" We haven't lived spiritually until we can walk as Jesus ... we can do that.

In 1970 God called both of us to go into Christian ministry as pastors. The "call" for me happened like this: One evening I sat down to read the Bible and turned to the little book of Titus that I'd never read before. As I was reading the first chapter and finished verses 6 through 9, I heard a voice say "That's you." I read it twice more and heard the same thing. I was sitting by the desk when the phone rang. It was the "well-to-do" owner of the large dairy farm across the fence from me. One time I had asked him what it took to acquire a million dollars. He said: "Oh I don't worry about dollars ... now, pennies, that's a different thing." He had purchased bulls from me, and we chatted a couple minutes when he said that he had a friend from out of state that was interested in finding a farm in our neighborhood that his friend might buy, and have Mr. Kleiner's manager run it. I didn't really need any affirmation about the call to preach, but this was unbelievable. We talked and agreed on a price.

All night and the next morning I was thinking about how to sell the top-quality herd that had been developed. As I came in for breakfast, the phone rang with a call from another dairyman, Jerry Dirkson, that frequently bought cows from me that didn't quite fit with my program. He rejoiced with me to hear I would be going into pastoral ministry and then asked if he might buy the cows, because he had just finished building larger corrals. I was reluctant because I was planning for immediate cash, and I knew that it would have to be a monthly payment. Long story short, my mind accepted, and the deal was made. So in about 12 hours most of my operations sale had been agreed upon. Deals that I'd had no thought of happening 24 hours earlier.

Not everyone was happy about this whole event. I was buying the farm from my parents, who expected me to run the farm and eventually pass it on to my son. They were so upset that they wanted to break our purchase agreement, and when that wouldn't work they consulted a lawyer to see if I could be put in an institution. Insane asylum, it was called.

That really hurt, but in a few days during a time of Bible reading, I came across Mark 10:29–31: "'Truly I tell you,' Jesus replied, 'no one who has left home or brothers or sisters or mother or father or children or fields for me and the gospel will fail to receive a hundred times as much in this present age: homes, brothers, sisters, mothers, children and fields—along with persecutions—and in the age to come eternal life. But many who are first will be last, and the last first.'"

That really struck home—God was again talking directly to me, it seemed. It all seemed to be exactly right, especially the part about the provision of homes. Dad had told me that as pastors we would never have a decent home to live in. But God said we would, so here is what has happened in regard to homes.

When we arrived in Colorado Springs, the new home we found was in our price range, and all the amenities we could ever want. It was built by a carpenter who would build a house and live in it for a while and get the bugs worked out and then sell it. How convenient! The location was also perfect for going to college, but more than that, there was nothing but open ground to see from our breakfast table. There was a hundred yards of undeveloped land before a road crossed, and immediately beyond that was Palmer Park—a big city park. We had always lived in places where the nearest neighbor was at least a quarter mile away, but can you believe, God knew our emotional needs. It also "happened" that we had wonderful neighbors on each side of us ten feet away.

The move to our first church to pastor took us to Los Alamos, New Mexico. They didn't have a parsonage, so we had to buy a home. We hadn't become wealthy when we sold the farm, but it did "just happen" to enable us to acquire a wonderful home that was just finishing construction, and Norma, my artist wife, got to choose all the colors inside and out. Empty lots all around. It was perfect.

A few years later we received a surprise call to a church in our home area of Idaho. We prayed about that because there is an old saying that goes something like "A prophet is without honor in his home area." But it seemed right and some leaders said, "Well, it is because you have a good reputation that they want you."

We accepted without ever seeing the people or the parsonage, and when we arrived we discovered that they would provide a large home, paved parking area with basketball hoop, three-car garage, large sand play area for children behind the garage, massive old productive black walnut tree, and a sheep pasture across the fence outside our living-room window. Besides that, it was just a short walk to a stream with some terrific trout fishing. It was a joy to serve there, and the church was able to purchase a small acreage to build a new sanctuary. It wasn't all heavenly, but seemed close most of the time.

We had other comfortable places in Spokane, Auckland, New Zealand; Santa Clara, CA; and with more adjectives, retirement homes; and finally a fine facility called Wind Crest for several thousand retirees. Dad said we would suffer, God said, "No you won't." Remember, this is all the story of a man for whom abortion was avoided.

PHOTO ALBUM

EACH SNAPSHOT HAS A STORY

Me in uniform. Supply Staff Sgt AF/ANG 1951- 1954
Moody Air Force Base, Valdosta GA
George AFB, Victorville, CA
Gowen Field, Boise ID

PHOTO ALBUM

Daughter-in-law Melinda and son Jeff outside the 1880 house with turret that he restored in Colorado Springs

Me teaching in Vacation Bible School for perhaps 60 children, many of them from Moslem families

My grandson Nate and Jeff at Vanguard high school graduation a week before Jeff died.

A going away banquet for Pastors Ray & Norma

PHOTO ALBUM

Don Jacinde's 1953 "new" Plymouth after he rolled it on Labor Day weekend 1953 between Boise & Mt. Home. Neither he nor Raymond were seriously injured, though Raymond had a back problem the rest of his life. The car rolled 7 times at 80 MPH. There were no seatbelts.

Danny Garcia

The first of three cars I was riding in that were totaled. The only injury was to my back. There were no seat belts in 1953. In 1978 my pickup rolled and in 2012 my car was crushed as I waited for a light to change.

CONCEIVABLE

Colorado Springs Police recognize years of chaplain service

**Crestline Church of the Nazarene
where where we were pastors from 1986-1992**

PHOTO ALBUM

Fishing in Colorado mountain beaver pond.

Catching
my favorite
eating…
Black Crappie

43

Holstein bull wins national recognition

Lazy L Skyliner Wally led by his breeder and half one by Ray Lane. Grand Champion at the San Francisco Cow Palace and Honorable mention All-American

Part of the holstein herd that was the highest producing for two years in the early "70s

PHOTO ALBUM

Serving communion outside the empty tomb.
We also did some baptisms in the Jordan River Preaching

Preaching in the "Good Friday" service at Wind Crest 2023

CONCEIVABLE

Daugther Leah, massage specialist extraordinaire, and husband Lee, satelite telecommunications expert.

Artist Norma at work with a favorite friend and favorite items in her 1,700 painting sold

"Madonna & Child" (Mary and baby Jesus)
Norma Lane 1936 - 2011
(suitable for 5x7 framing)

5
POSSIBLE (41–69)

Now, quick return back to college. We had been out of school for 18 years, so it concerned us about how we would do academically. We had failed to take into account the fact that we had been in a strong church, operating a small business, and getting graduate studies on humanities all the time. When the three years were up, we graduated second and third in our class.

There were seven invitations of where we might go to be pastors. East and South didn't seem like where God could best use Western farm descendants of pioneers. The classes were challenging and glorious with awesome professors. Some theology (the study of God and religious belief) classes were daunting, but it was like the glory of God was ever-present.

Norma was involved in teaching fine art and poster making aside from study. My jobs included being elected to fill a spot on a council that worked between the trustees and faculty to establish some overall direction for some operations of the college that had only been open for four years. Then for two years, the job of recording activities on film was mine … the photographer. I got accused of having a very ugly belly button because students never saw me without the camera hanging from my neck. The senior year, the job of yearbook editor was a big challenge. Somehow there was time to learn to play golf with two of the professors almost every Thursday afternoon at Patty Jewett Golf Course. I worked some for Ward's as an installer, but the sale of the farm had taken care of school costs, while most of the other students had to work full time and go to classes that were given both day and evening.

I suppose working an average of 70 hours a week on the farm was also good preparation for whatever was next ... though when people ask what work I did, my answer is always, "I never had to work, I always enjoyed where God had put me."

The actual assignment of being a pastor never has a dull moment, and some days are painful. Then there are days like the first Pentecost Sunday that we were in Los Alamos, our first assignment. The worship service was going well and I had planned a bit of drama to open my message. The first words out of my mouth were "IF THERE IS ANYTHING MAN WANTS, IT'S **POWER!!!**" Immediately there was an explosive **KA-BOOM** and the entire building shook. Lightning had struck right outside. It was the beginning of a typical New Mexico storm. Still being "a little wet behind the ears," I tried to continue the well-prepared message when I should have just said "AMEN" and adjourned.

I always thought pastors were likely to get calls in the middle of the night, so for years I had a red phone by the bed in case someone needed help at night ... it never, ever rang. Once I said to one of the PhDs there in Los Alamos, "Sometimes I feel a bit intimidated by all the geniuses around here." He said, "Oh don't worry about that, we know a lot about quantum physics and protons, atoms and chemistry. What we need from you is to get to the place where we know the Creator and His Son better." I said, "We can do that," and we did to a significant degree. Whenever we moved to a new place, I announced to the congregation that at least every other week Norma would preach in the morning; they would hear a really good message, because she would preach one week and me the next. (I guess I was okay too.) That was the way we handled our preaching most of the time, and she was a powerfully strong preacher with a special ministry to "healing for damaged emotions." She had some dynamic ministries in places and churches besides the ones where we pastored.

Los Alamos, being the home of the atomic bombs, was a highly spiritual place. I was told that as far as anyone knew there was only one atheist in town. The idea of all the deaths that were caused by Hiroshima and Nagasaki to end WWII was never a happy thought. From the time of the bombs until now, much of the research has been directed to working toward cancer treatments.

One time a call came that there was a prisoner in the New Mexico state prison that a man needed a pastor to visit. I'm not sure how my name came up, but a man had been convicted and sent to prison for murdering his wife and children. I went twice to see him. Now, even forty-five years later, the man is still stamped in my mind. He was afraid to take a shower, and hadn't for months. He was afraid that if he went in the shower he would be killed. At that time even convicted felons had standards, and killing a child, especially his own, went beyond what they would tolerate. A couple months after my second visit, there was an announcement in the paper of a death in the prison … it was him. There was never word of an investigation. I never learned of his eternal destination.

One of the surprises of ministry for us was that we didn't find a lot of theological questions, as the most common needs concerned money and sex. After we had left our first church, we asked our district leader if he had ever received any complaints about our preaching. He thought for a bit and then said yes.

"Once someone said, 'the Lanes seem to always preach something about holiness.'" I did a fist pump on that one. We preach from the Holy Bible about a God who wants His people to be holy.

Apparently our preaching and the weekly Bible studies that we conducted were reasonably good for maturing all of us. I wrote something over 400 weekly studies based on the previous week's message so everyone could discuss any questions. Those small group studies covered about everything you can imagine.

As I look back over my ministry, there are a few scriptures in the Bible that kind of stand out; this is not to indicate that everything from Genesis to Revelation is less important. But the universally known verse is John 3:16: "For God so loved the world that he gave his one and only Son, that whoever believes in him shall not perish but have eternal **life**." Because the Bible is a very special book written to each of us personally, I have often asked people to put their name in where appropriate when reading. For instance, put my name in place of whoever; put "that Ray believes (I do) and will have eternal **life**." John 10:10b says, "I have come that they (you and me) may have **life** and have it in the full." Notice that Jesus says … he is talking to each of us. Are we listening to the promised fact that he has a quality, satisfying life in the spirit for each of us?

When doing podcast interviews as I did for two years, my key question was always, "You have lived many years as a believer, would you describe your life as okay?" Most people could hardly stop giving an answer. The planned twelve-minute interview more often went over twenty minutes.

Then in John 14:26, Jesus on the night before he was to die was comforting his disciples and says, "But the advocate, the Holy Spirit whom the Father will send in my name, will teach **you** all things and will remind **you** of everything I have said to you." Do we fully understand that he is speaking to every believer? Will you think of all the teaching and reminding that is ever present? If that isn't clear, then you are blind like I was for so long. Also, John the beloved writes in I John 3:6, "Whoever remains in Him (continues believing) does not sin. Whoever sins has not seen Him and does not know Him." And in I John 5:18–19 we find, "We know that whoever is one of God does not keep on sinning. But whoever has been born of God guards himself, and the wicked one cannot touch him. We know that we are of God, and the whole world lies in wickedness." Surely that is clear to you. There is a clear illustration of believers not continuing in sin in John 8:1–11 about the woman caught in adultery. At the end of this situation, Jesus says to her, "go and sin no more." A Christian does not go on sinning; it would be nice if he never made a mistake, which is a different thing and unavoidable. The biblical definition of sin as put together by John Wesley is: "Sin is a willful transgression (choice) against the known will of God." Christianity is not a sinning life, but a clean life in every way. If it wasn't possible as Jesus indicated in these scriptures, he wouldn't have said so.

While our first pastorate was in a new church, our second in Kuna, Idaho (old home country), was an old church but had a lot of young couples, both farmers and people that commuted to cities like Boise and Nampa. It is amazing how each church has its own character—mostly good.

Among the many good times, one of the most interesting memories in Kuna was that one Easter we had an overflow crowd with some people having to stand; they didn't complain, but it was embarrassing. I must have lost my train of thought, because, with the largest crowd ever, I forgot to take an offering. A special blessing came one Thanksgiving when I delivered a full dinner to an elderly lady that lived in a house that really didn't stop all the wind. She said she didn't want to come to church because she literally didn't have anything to wear. But when I was getting up to leave, she said "just a minute"—she pressed a 50-dollar bill into my hand and said, "I am so thankful that Jesus is my savior, I've been saving for this." Our church always gave money for the worldwide preaching of the gospel. We'd done a few things for her and her brother, but I cried as I realized that we had never given enough to help her. It was truly the widow's mite.

While we were in Kuna, an opportunity came for me to make the first of two trips to Israel—the place all Christians want to visit. The trip started with flying to Kennedy Airport in New York, where we waited six hours for our Royal Jordanian 747 plane to be de-iced twice before we could get in the air at 1 a.m. Four hours later by our time, we were awakened for our morning coffee. My seat mate and I asked for some, so we received a couple of small cups, and when the steward poured my friend's "coffee," it went *plop*. I quickly said, "No thanks." I was then told that Jordanian coffee was a small amount of well-brewed stuff that was to be followed by a lot of milk. They really like it that way.

Anyway, since we were behind schedule we didn't land in Amman, Jordan, until 11 p.m. their time. Walking down the concourse in the terminal was interesting. The passengers from that flight were the only people in the hall passing between two rows of soldiers holding their M-15s at parade rest. Believe me, nobody stepped out of line. Since everyone on that flight was a tourist, we were all moved by buses and booked into a nice hotel where they had set up a buffet at 6 p.m. on a group of tables loaded with perhaps 80 food items ... "cool," but nothing hot ... like it would have been five hours earlier.

In the gift shop I purchased a red and white keffiyeh, and was wearing it the next morning when we passed over the Allenby Bridge to enter Israel. One of the border guards suggested that I might be better off not to wear that headgear because he said I looked a lot like Arafat.

The sightseeing was incredible as we saw all the well-known sites. I had the privilege of preaching on Mount Carmel where Elijah had confronted all the priests of Baal. Then I baptized several believers in the Jordan River just below the Sea of Galilee. I wonder if my siblings in heaven witnessed that event? Maybe I'll find out soon enough. When we visited a shop with wood carvings of olive wood, I bought enough wooden communion cups to use in serving communion several times when I got home. They always gave an opportunity to emphasize Jesus' death because the grape juice left a crimson stain in the wooden cups. Then I also held a communion service in the garden by the empty tomb. An incredible blessing of God for all of us. Some things you never forget.

After a few fruitful years, we began to think about New Zealand because that had been one of the places that had offered us a call when we graduated from Bible college. After about six years in Kuna, a denomination leader of our church, the Church of the Nazarene, called us and said that there were two churches in Auckland that were without pastors—could we come? Norma for New Linn and me for Auckland First Church of the Nazarene. It would mean that the churches would have to prove that no one was available in their country to fill the positions. And then that we would have to pay our own way. The second part was solved by the fact that Norma was fairly well known and an accomplished artist by now. She had a sale and raised enough money to pay for the journey … this woman that had her husband reluctantly pay for Norman Rockwell lessons.

So we flew south of the equator into tomorrow on the other side of the international date line. Where we had to drive on the opposite side of the road. Norma never could sit up and look ahead while we were driving. We only came close to having an accident a couple of times. One when two cars were racing, and on a two-lane road we were passed at the same time on both sides.

But one of the things this survivor of abortion knows is that it is wonderful to be able to be in a place where you are needed and be able to make a difference. Both of our assigned churches had had some very difficult problems in the past and we were able to help. The people of "down under" are wonderful.

In one situation of ministry there was a middle-aged Maori lady that was bedfast and must have weighed 400+ pounds, but she still had a prayer ministry from bed. We visited her several times, did a baby dedication there, and were blessed by this lady and her family. We heard that about five years later God healed her and she was able to get up, live a normal life, and get married.

Another Maori family became good friends and invited us over for dinner. In fun, we asked what the main course would be, because two hundred years ago the native population made a practice of cannibalism and some of the first missionaries suffered that fate. The museums all have samples of the unique forks that had been used to eat flesh. In time Christian principles were followed and family is extremely important where mostly matriarchal (women dominate) practices prevail.

There are many small pointed hills that came from volcanic eruptions and were said to be places where witches' covens met.

One of their favorite activities was to put a cross of a couple of white lilies in your driveway most Sunday mornings. We were told that this was their way of telling us pastors that they were praying to Satan for us to die.

Our return to the States happened because the health-care system in New Zealand, while very good for small problems like a bad sliver or a broken finger.. But anything that required hospitalization was often very difficult because of strikes and shortages of workers at all levels. While the people wanted us to stay longer, it would have required our return to the States and enduring a year of red tape.

One day we read in the paper that a man had been waiting eleven months to get his kidney stones removed. I'd had kidney stones twice and death would have been preferable to waiting that long, so we stayed to the end of our visa and came to where treatment would be available if needed. Eight years later another stone event happened, so I was glad to be home.

We were without assignment at that time, so we contacted some district superintendents of our church. We had visited a church in Spokane, and another in Vici, Oklahoma, and were in a bit of a quandary about which place God wanted us to be. Both were in need of pastors, they liked us, and we liked both congregations. We met God in prayer, and like what happened in the book of Acts with Saul (who became the apostle Paul), God let us know that we would fit well in either place for Him. Anyway, as we were visiting Vici, the church building was very nice and we went next door to visit a pleasant parsonage that would be available for us. One part of the viewing took us downstairs. We entered a room with no windows and our guide said, "This would be your tornado shelter." Norma leaned over and whispered in my ear, "I hear Spokane calling!" Westerners like us had heard of Tornado Alley, but actually living there caused our cowardice to take over. Besides, our adventuresome son had sent us a picture one time that he had taken by leaning out of a dormitory window and said, "This is what the middle of a tornado looks like from the bottom just before it touched down on the other side of the building in Olathe, Kansas."

So, God led us to Spokane Crestline, a church on the edge of the inner city. We had seven years of effective ministry there with lots of memories. One good one was being called to visit an elderly widow that had a small, nicely kept home but obviously had a lot of struggles, but, oh how she loved God. After visiting for a while, she said she had something she wanted to give me. It was $1,000 made out to our missionary society for the purpose of bringing the gospel to the world. (These awesome events of love tributes that the world may sneer at bear repeating.) She not only blessed us, she blessed the world, and we saw firsthand a sacrifice that pleased God. She never went hungry, and her funeral later was a true celebration of LIFE.

That was also where we experienced law enforcement in action. One day I saw a man jump the fence at the side of our house, run across the yard, and then some shouting. I stepped out in the backyard to see a policeman tackle the man. I went to see if help was needed, but the officer was sitting on the back of a man that had a warrant out for his arrest. That was soon all cleared away. Then one Sunday morning as I crossed the back lawn from the parsonage to the church, I was surprised to see that the driver of the church van to pick up children for Sunday school had gone out a little early. It turned out that the church had been vandalized, my office broken into, keys found, and the van stolen. The thieves must have spent hours hammering on the church safe to get it open, only to find it empty. There was also the morning one of our seniors called and asked if the pastor (me) could come to the police station and take him home, as he had spent the night there. It was all a misunderstanding, but a visit to a judge happened as a result.

A call came that several churches in the San Francisco area were in need of a pastor. We prayed and felt that an old farm boy from Idaho might not fit at San Francisco First Church of the Nazarene, but rather that Santa Clara in the Silicon Valley might be more appropriate in part because of working with PhDs in Los Alamos, New Mexico. It would be eight years of what pastors call a honeymoon assignment. Of course there are always thorns in the midst of roses. There were several opportunities to visit the Santa Clara County detention center and the San Jose jail and court. A member of one of our families had a knack for breaking the laws about drugs. While the actual jailhouse visits seemed meaningful sitting in a cell or talking to someone behind glass, the exercise of sometimes walking among the muscle-building prisoners was unsettling. Another surprise to me was that when waiting to visit a prisoner, there would be some of the most beautiful women waiting to see their man. Some of those times were a bit like sitting with the ten finalists of the Miss America Pageant waiting to be seen on stage.

Another relatively unique ministry developed there. I began to conduct grief-remembrance services for families whose pets had died. The first was with a young couple whose pet rabbit had died. Later there were services for families whose cats, dogs, and a canary had died.

One illustration that I always used was about a man by the name of Bill that I talked to several times. He is a retired policeman with a health problem. One year, in spite of being warned not to go out in the mountains alone, he decided to take his muzzleloader rifle and go elk hunting. On this trip he was on a mountainside and had a seizure. He had medicine for it, but was unable to get to it. He lay incapacitated on the hillside in the heavy forest of central Colorado. He could comprehend his situation, but could do nothing about it. He was of course concerned about the coldness of the September night ahead when the temperature could easily get to freezing. But when darkness fell, four cow elk came and lay down next to him and kept him warm. When the sun came up, the cows left. He could hear searchers looking for him the next day, but they never found him. When darkness arrived, so did the four cow elk to keep him warm a second night. The next day the searchers found him. I have spoken to him several times. He says he has given up elk hunting and so have many others that have heard his story. There are numerous stories of animals that are God's creation as well as man seemingly being directed by God. (There is a massive amount of ink that has been spilled surrounding this kind of event and I could go there, but this book is about one man's experiences ... me.)

All in all, though, we loved living and being ministers in the Silicon Valley.

The Christian church is struggling to connect to our younger generation and perhaps a deeper awareness of the awesome fact of God's desire to affect every moral action of our lives, which whether in word, thought, or deed can have a positive connection to those operating on feelings as they find this personal relationship to One who truly loves them. Besides, as someone has said, "We are earthly beings in a spiritual world."

In our first church as pastors, we called retired missionary

Rev. Elmer Schmelzenbaugh to come and hold meetings with us and another church. The morning he was to fly from Oklahoma City to Albuquerque, my phone rang. It was Elmer, who said, "I can't come, the airport is fogged in and no planes are taking off." I said, "Oh Elmer, this is terrible, we have done so much work and prayer in preparation." He said, "Well they are not flying." I blurted out, not thinking that I was talking to a giant of the faith, "Elmer, you head for the airport and I'll pray." Just as I hit my knees to pray, I "heard" the title of an old hymn, "It's Just Like Jesus to Roll the Clouds Away." I said, "Thanks, Lord," and headed for the car to drive two hours to the airport. These were in the days before cell phones. Those hours between hearing the "voice" and seeing Elmer forever added to my always deepening faith and trust in God. I remember that while I was waiting to see if Elmer was there, I had some anxiety, perhaps like doubting Thomas. Looking back, I was reminded of the time when God had called me into ministry and my parents thought I'd lost my mind and actually tried to get me to a psychiatrist. But when the plane landed, Elmer got off and our joy was unlimited. He then told me that there was a time when the sky cleared and they took off … the only one that morning. We had great services!

Any time we get a word from Him (in whatever form it happens), it will have a scriptural backing—always. We are the temple of the Holy Spirit (I Col. 6:19) and have access to the mind of Christ or He to us, but there are two other "voices" to contend with … me, myself & I (that's one) and, on occasions, perhaps some very unkind or evil thoughts that come from the enemy of our soul. We will always need discernment to be absolutely clear as to the source. Also, there is Isaiah 55:8–9: "'For my thoughts are not your thoughts, neither are your ways my ways,' declares the Lord. 'As the heavens are higher than the earth, so are my ways higher than your ways and my thoughts than your thoughts (NIV).'" The fact that He gives *me* his thoughts is both humbling and exciting.

In searching to find a closing illustration to try to describe how the Comforter enters into our brain (mind), one of the possibilities can be found in Luke 1:35 where He says to Mary, "the Holy Spirit will come upon you and the power of the most high will overshadow you." What did Mary say when told that she would have baby Jesus (short story)? … "let it be so"! It's a mystery in both cases that we can't seem to explain (faith?), but remember how with the apostle Paul, God spoke one very special personal time to him: "Saul, Saul, why do you persecute me?" And we are told about it three times. Why should we be so hesitant to proclaim the marvelous communications of God? After all, He is a God of miracles. We might add Ezekiel 37:14 that says: "I will put My Spirit within you and you will come to life" (NASB). Then Philippians 2:5 says, "Your attitude (mind) should be the same as Christ Jesus." The KJ says, "LET this mind be in you that is in Christ Jesus." Now, what does that little three-letter word mean? One main meaning of let is "allow" … what does that mean? It means that I have a choice to make. If I let my teen use the car, it is a big choice. LETTING the mind of Christ be in me means that I allow Him to take over. It means we trust God. When Mary said let it be to me and the Holy Spirit "moved in," a baby was born by trust in God. We have to take action and ALLOW Him to take over. It may seem like using disconnected scriptures, but when there are so many, the consensus grows.

As you are reading or listening to this, perhaps you are thinking that you'd like to hear from God … wonderful. It <u>can</u> and should happen! But please know that the way this happens is not by seeking to hear a voice, but by seeking the One who does the speaking ... JESUS! He is behind this and all the many other aspects of our relationship: the forgiveness of our sins, abundant life now and forever with Him. How wonderful ... Praise His Holy Name, and may He richly bless you as you ALLOW the creator of all the earth to "speak" ... perhaps you will listen closer!!!

On Easter weekend 2000, we had invited best friend and mentor Al and wife Kitty Jones to visit and to be involved in the Sunday worship in Santa Clara. But the night before, it became necessary for me to take Norma to the hospital because of an atrial fibrillation heart problem. This had happened a couple times before when an allergic reaction to some chemical would bring about a time of knocking her heart out of rhythm. I called Al from the hospital at seven in the morning and told him that the Easter worship service was theirs to conduct. God directed in an excellent worship time.

But this time recovery for Norma was much more difficult and required several days in the hospital. When she returned home, we began to think that our time to retire from our pastoral duties had arrived. Like many people, we had anticipated that day coming, just not so soon. A few years before, on a trip to visit our son and family in Colorado Springs, we had looked for and found just the right house, which we'd purchased and found an excellent renter for in expectation of retiring in 2002. As we were praying about it, we came across a scripture that said, "return to the country of your family." So we announced to the church that we would be retiring at the end of August so that they could begin their process of locating whoever would follow us.

So, now we were planning to retire, but we had a renter

that was supposed to get a thirty-day notice. I was about to call them, but Norma said, let's wait a week or two. We had lived by the Spirit's prompting for many years, so this was not too unusual a way to hear from Him. Within a week the renter called and said, "I have some bad news. My job is moving me to Albuquerque, and I have to be there on July 5th." I told him that he had been the best a renter could be, and that a pay raise for him and an empty house for me was actually a win-win event. So, on the Fourth of July I loaded a car with my big old radial-arm saw from the farm and other tools in the car and drove to Colorado Springs to spend two weeks doing some minor remodeling. When that was finished a friend drove me to the airport to return to Santa Clara. One car was left in Colorado at the house that was empty for a month. I know that as a pastor I should not be surprised that life events just seem to happen. Even though he said, "Lo, I will always be with you." I never cease to wonder why it isn't always that way for everyone. (Or perhaps it is.) I believe that the care he had given before I was born is scheduled to continue to happen all my days … both for my life and those that are touched by Him through my life.

Any move has some emotional highpoint and low points. There is an old saying that three home moves is the equivalent to a fire. We had thought we had been careful enough with adding to our "stuff," but it became evident that we were going to have to make some tough decisions. This was the first of four "downsizings" that would happen to me. The last move to where I am now was made by stuffing the back of my medium-sized SUV. That was tough and terrific at the same time.

Occasionally when a pastor moves away there may be a sigh of relief that they are gone, but our relationship there was like a very close family. It was like a time when the kids move out to go to college. This time there were a lot of tears on all sides. We left knowing that the church was on solid ground financially, but most important was that the Creator God who is Love was on the throne of most every heart.

Labor Day was on Monday that year, and we managed with help from many friends and our son that had flown out to make the two-day drive to Colorado. We had the truck ready to hit the road on Saturday morning. Norma was taken to the airport with kitty in carrier, and we got in line with thousands of others to "get out of Dodge" on a holiday weekend. The fact that traffic was slow was probably a good thing for us. Since I still had farm instincts for truck driving, I took the first few hours. For some reason the freeway surface seemed rough all the way, like there was a joint in the concrete every thirty feet, so that most of the way it was *pound, bump, pound*. The truck was like … *well like riding in a truck.* We had the feeling that when we finally opened the back door at our destination, the whole load would just run out like sand. One time when we stopped, we checked to see if the car on the dolly towed by the truck was okay and discovered that only one of the two front tires was fastened down: the harness over the other tire had come off. Literally, God only knows how far we drove like that with the possibility of a massive tragedy existing.

Jeff had exactly 0 hours behind the steering wheel of a truck. He did well all across Nevada until we pulled into a motel parking lot in Bonneville Flats, Utah. I went in the office to get us checked in, and just as that was finishing Jeff came in looking sheepish, and said, "Dad, we have a problem. Come and see." It turned out that the parking lot was full … races on the salt flats the next day, of course. He had started to try to drive around through the lot when he discovered that there was no way to make the turn to come out. So, it was my job to back a large truck with car on dolly behind out of the lot, since there was no space to get the car off the dolly. Years before on the farm during harvest, I learned to back a single front-tire tractor, pulling an offset two-wheel hay chopper, with four-wheel enclosed hay wagon behind that … It's hard to imagine, but I was pretty accomplished at it … no sweat, really.

Anyway, with a little direction from outside by Jeff, the whole outfit made it out of the lot with no paint lost so it could be parked on the street. We could never have imagined the terror we would experience the next evening.

The drive across Nevada and western Colorado was without incident until after we had stopped at Idaho Springs to have a bite. When we got back on I-70 going down into Denver, it was all downhill which was okay for a while, but not being an experienced truck driver, Jeff did not shift down to a lower gear to hold us back; as we began to pick up speed, he began depending on the brakes until they burned out. We were afraid to try to shift down because if it didn't work, we would have been totally freewheeling. So we ended up coasting at 80 mph clear on to I 470 for what we would guess was 20 to 25 miles or so of coasting before we were able to stop. Fortunately it was Sunday evening and most people were where they planned to stay before they came home Monday, so the traffic was as light as it was ever likely to be. Still, the cars we whizzed past in our truck with car in tow must have shocked some people. We miraculously coasted to a stop to let the brakes cool off. The waiting time was also used to let our racing hearts go back to normal, and then we made the final miles very slowly to Colorado Springs with hazard lights blinking. Neither of us would ever get behind the wheel of a truck again after that trip.

When we arrived at the nice little retirement home, we found a large pile of carpet out in the front yard. I said, "Norma,

WHAT HAVE YOU DONE?" Well it turned out that the little room attached to the garage wouldn't be large enough for her to continue painting … that activity that her husband had thought was something she could do in retirement. She continued painting and teaching for about eight years, doing some extraordinary work. The carpet had come out of the master bedroom when she and Melinda, our daughter-in-law, had pulled up a corner of the rug and discovered a beautiful hardwood floor. This turned out to be the room where the painting where Madonna & Child was painted. We had planned on sleeping in separate bedrooms anyway, since we had done that for years because of my lifelong loud snoring problem.

When we had started pastoral ministry, it was an unusual event to have both husband and wife pastor together, and we called ourselves co-pastors and others would call us Pastor Ray and Pastor Norma. We had spoken with the man in charge of pensions for the worldwide Church of the Nazarene, and he told us our time of service would be that each of us would get credit for our years of service just like a senior pastor and assistant pastor would be credited. Well, when we applied to get whatever the amount would be for our years on assignment, the word came back to us that we would only receive one pension. We said, "You mean to say that each of us is only half a person?" Well that started a lot of letters with church leaders that knew us saying that wasn't right; but unfortunately while we agree with you, headquarters has a handbook that says that is the way they must act. So a rule change was submitted to our General Assembly that met once every four years and a resolution went through process, and it was fixed so that we not only got our pension, but so has every couple that has had the same arrangement since then. It has now become fairly common, so with God's help, something happened that was good for many out of my life.

Since we were both called of God to be pastors, had testimonies to prove that, and had gone through all the necessary years of education and experience, we were ordained together in Clovis, New Mexico, in 1977 while we were pastors in Los Alamos. Our ministry form that we adopted was that we would share the Sunday morning preaching. We experimented with sharing the same message, but it seemed we were more effective if she preached one week and me the next. In one interview we had, we were asked how we planned to function; looking at me, the question was asked, "Will you be the senior pastor and she the children's pastor?" I said, "Unlikely—since she is a powerful preacher I would want her as senior pastor and I'd probably be the children's pastor." The process ended up with the preaching going as described. I handled all the administration and other services, as well as leading a small group during the week. If there was a man that needed to talk to a pastor, that was my job. Women with needs were Norma's responsibility. We really were two full-time pastors!

The idea of women being biblically qualified to teach and preach has often been of concern, then and now. So before we ever went to a church we did some teaching about the issue. Only once in our years did we have a man visit and then not come to church for that reason … that was his problem. But because the issue continued so that everyone in the church needed to understand the Church of the Nazarene and many other denominations employed women in pastoral ministry, I handed a position paper to everyone telling people why the Church of the Nazarene and many other denominations approve women in ministry. It mentioned the Old Testament leadership of the judge Deborah, and leadership roles of Esther and Ruth. In Acts 18 Paul lists Aquila first and Priscilla second, then later it becomes her first and him second. They were leaders much like my wife and I. Also, when the gifts of the spirit were described, there was no indication that male or female entered in. All gifts were available to all. A little study will show that the places where Paul said women should be quiet or not lead were specific to individual situations. For instance, for the most part churches were meeting in homes with men on one side of the gathering and women on the other. The leader would be speaking, and when the women did not understand something they would speak across the aisle to say, "What is he saying?" It was disruptive and Paul says, "Stop it." Also, not that it makes any difference, but a number of theologians think that it is possible that a woman could have written the book of Hebrews.

The thought of being retired generally has the concept of being idle or being on vacation, but in my case, it seems that my accomplishments in the recent years may have benefited society in many ways.

Soon after getting settled and having a few days of getting up in the morning without something to do, I decided to see what was open to me. After all, 68 isn't all that old. After a couple of unsatisfying jobs, a friend suggested that a number of pastors in my position were employed by funeral homes. One day there was an interview with a lady funeral director. She said they didn't need anyone at the moment, but at 7 the next morning she called and said we need you in an hour. It was just to be a helper that day at a funeral. My job meant opening doors and moving flowers. I was to ride with an experienced driver in a limousine to pick up a family and take them to the service and then to the cemetery later, and home. Well, it so happened that a blizzard was going on that January day. The driver said he knew a shortcut to the family home. (Are you ready for this?) The street he chose had a stop sign at the top of a very small hill. Well, we stopped okay, but the snow had picked up enough that it was solid ice … we were stuck! Limousines are notorious for being useless on ice. A few tries were unsuccessful, so he was able to back up to a main road and get turned around. Then we tried another street, only to find it closed for utility work. The third try was the charm, and we arrived to pick up the family that was out in the street screaming at us because the service a few miles away was supposed to have already started. My first day turned out to be good instruction on how not to do a job … that is a good thing for an employee.

The next week the funeral director called again. Her full crew was occupied and the body of an elderly deceased lady was waiting to be collected and brought to the funeral home. Okay. The frail lady was in an upstairs bedroom of a really old house. There was no room to put the body on a stretcher, so a young experienced man and I had to wrestle her out of the room to the top of a narrow stairway to get her down to a gurney to transfer her to the hearse. I'm not entirely sure which is the most difficult problem: dealing with a body in rigor mortis or recent, still warm bodies. I was told that if she had weighed several hundred pounds we would have had a real problem. Anyway, we got her to the back of the funeral home and a small room downstairs by elevator to the room where embalming was to happen.

Now, this old pastor who had always thought that the body in a casket was appropriate for a funeral suddenly discovered embalming. We put the body on a table and the boss described the process that isn't terribly complicated, but means performing a significant operation. She said that I didn't have to do it if I chose not to; someone else could take care of it. I chose NO. If we have to mess with the body anyway, maybe cremation is an acceptable idea.

This event led me to write the following pamphlet about cremation that has been placed in many funeral homes and read by probably a thousand families.

HELPFUL THOUGHTS ABOUT CREMATION

Most people are familiar with burial, but many do not know what to think about cremation. This is for those who are interested in discovering what the Bible has to say about this choice.

WHAT TO DO? The Bible tells us in I Corinthians that our last enemy, death, has been defeated. That is true of course if we understand that eternal life follows the temporary life we have on earth. For Bible believers who grieve, this is a genuine comfort.

But there is a choice that we must make when a loved one dies. "What do we do with this earthly body?" For many people, that choice is like facing an enemy in battle that leaves you with no way out, and we may think that no matter what we choose, we lose. This body is the vessel that has housed the personality and creativity and has been significant from its beginning. We have cared for it, loved through it, and spent money on it in multitudes of ways and all that is in the past. But now we are faced with how we are to dispose of it.

For those who accept the Bible as God's word to live (and die) by, there is a desire to know what God thinks is the best procedure to follow. This pamphlet is presented simply to provide some insight into the theological aspects of the acceptability of cremation. Scholars will likely always differ as to what choice to make. But it is interesting to note that Roman Catholics have deemed cremation to be acceptable. Some people, whether Roman Catholic or not, have felt that that position held great weight and was therefore worthy to be followed. The church position was based on Canon Law more than directly on Scripture, and the recent change is simply in response to Catholic pastoral needs.

THE WORD SAYS ...

So what does the Bible say about cremation? Well, nothing ... at least the word "cremation" does not appear in most versions, though there may be some new modern language versions that use the word.

Now the Bible is clear about many things. It does state that for believers, our body is "... the temple of the Holy Spirit" (I Col. 3:16). And "We are the temple of the living God" (II Corinthians. 6:16). Some say "because of that, we need to treat it with respect and therefore burial is the only way to go." If we think about what happens to the body in preparation for burial and feel that having the body take a long time to turn to dust is respectful, then that is probably the way to go. But if you think this process of being turned to dust taking a short time rather than years is respectful, then cremation is worth consideration. (Technically, the cremains are not dust, but rather the remains of bones.)

The Bible also says, "We are confident, I say, and willing rather to be absent from the body, and to be present with the Lord" (II Col. 5:8 KJV). It is obvious that the spiritual "body" has departed from the earthly body at death. It also says "It is sown a natural body, it is raised a spiritual body (soma pneumatikon)" (I Col. 15:44). Then, Hebrews 4:12 NASB says, "For the word of God is living and active and sharper than any two-edged sword, and piercing as far as the division of soul and spirit, of both joints and marrow." This clearly shows that our spirit is separate from the body and is freed to resurrection.

As far as the rapture of the body referred to in I Thessalonians 4, would it be any harder for God to assemble a glorified body from the ashes of the 9-11-01 destruction, or those lost at sea, or to bring John the Baptist's body and head together or in explosions or cremains, than it is to raise the dust of Christians who have been dead 2,000 years? (Again, we don't know exactly what the body is like that will "meet the Lord in the air" [Thessalonians 4:17].) Or for those who feel the need to have our present body and our future spiritual body connected, consider the fact that, in the beginning, God created our present physical body from the dust of the ground (Genesis 2:7). Would it be any more difficult for Him to give us a glorified body from our own dust?

Dr. Timothy George, *Christianity Today* Executive Editor and Dean of the Beeson Divinity School at Samford University, says, "… the Bible nowhere explicitly condemns cremation." And he says, "Billy Graham has noted (what Christians have always believed) that cremation cannot prevent a sovereign God from calling forth the dead at the end of time."

The Bible also tells us that life is in the blood that is circulating. But at death, life as we know it ends! It is clear that when a person does not see, hear, taste, smell, or feel anything, they are gone from this life. We no longer need to fear hurting or offending them. Their spiritual body is enjoying a separate existence.

Perhaps it should be said that in many areas of America there are more cremations than burials. Cremation does offer more options. You need to check on state laws, but usually cremains can be buried, displayed in a container, often in glass cases, and may be scattered or easily moved from place to place. No matter where traditional burial or cremation is chosen, those who grieve should have a time, usually public, to look back and also to look ahead. Beautiful, meaningful ceremonies can be arranged. Bringing a display of pictures, recreation items such as a fishing pole, a golf club, skis, a bowling ball, or items representing other life activities can be beautiful. Craft objects such as a quilt or clothing that have been created are useful in remembering life. So too are awards and certificates that commemorate work.

There was an interruption in my work after about a year. One day I had a doctor appointment to see what could be done about a lingering sore throat. After the examination and prescribing an antibiotic, the PA (physician's assistant) asked if I had any other problems. Well, the day before I had walked and played nine holes of golf and felt a little tired at the end and had a little tight feeling under where my tie would be. He said, "Let's do an EKG" (electrocardiogram), so that happened and he asked if I didn't have a cardiologist because I had hypertension (high blood pressure) medicine. He suggested I check with someone who had a record on me … he even called and set up another EKG for the next morning. After that test, the cardiologist said, "Well let's do a stress test." I felt fine, but why not. Soon after the stress test the doctor came and said, "We will do bypass surgery tomorrow. The weekend was coming so it couldn't be scheduled till Tuesday, but five bypasses happened that day. There was a problem when they pried me open in that a couple of ribs came out of place next to the vertebrae in the back. That pain was much worse than any kidney stone but settled down when the ribs got back in place a week later.

Anyway, I got out of the hospital on my 71st birthday and asked the doctor how long the procedure was good for. He said, "Well we used some new procedures, so we will find out when you die, but you are likely to die of some other problem." It's been over 20 years now, so he was probably right. In a couple of weeks I was back to work.

In the course of working as an assistant funeral director, I helped about a thousand families. Also, it provided the opportunity to minister to hurting families. Also, families without pastors provided an opportunity to serve during services over 200 times. It was truly a satisfying life activity for one that almost didn't have life.

Oh, there were some terribly emotional times, especially when a baby or small child was involved, or like when a fifteen-year-old cheerleader committed suicide in her father's clothes closet. Perhaps 1,500 mourners came to the service, where I was the presiding pastor.

Another particularly memorable time was when I was asked to preside in a service for a well-known MD who had passed away. As always in that situation, a family planning visit was in order and my meeting with the family was quite long and congenial. I was shown around the spacious home where every room held numerous heads of trophies of animals the doctor had brought home from all over the world. The next day I was greeting the full house in the chapel when referring to the pleasant family and I apparently had a brain freeze and said in appreciation of the family home, "That was the horniest house I've ever been in." There was a moment of deadly silence and then a roar of laughter. After the service the widow said, "That was awesome—when I die I want you to do my funeral!" That funeral director, however, never asked me to preside at his place again.

As I come to the end of my story, it seems to me that it is important to let you know part of the driving force behind writing this missive happened when the Colorado attorney general gave a report to the people of Wind Crest in August 2023 that is home for me now. He was asked what he thought of the Supreme Court's decision about Roe v. Wade. Essentially, his reply came by saying that he hoped people would come to their right mind and change it back. That made my blood boil. If he actually represented all the people of this state, he would recommend that half the tax money going to Planned Parenthood go to Right to Life groups. We will never keep abortions from happening, but the numbers could be cut way, way down. There are numerous agencies ready and able to help mothers-to-be, and a massive number of ways to help single mothers … just Google for help. NRLC is a good place to start.

I found this: Founded in 1968, National Right to Life is the nation's oldest and largest pro-life organization. National Right to Life is the federation of 50 state right-to-life affiliates and more than 3,000 local chapters. Through education and legislation, National Right to Life is working to restore legal protection to the most defenseless members of our society who are threatened by abortion, infanticide, assisted suicide, and euthanasia.

Abortion has existed from the time women discovered a way to terminate pregnancy—using many ways long before coat hangers. Obviously that was thousands of years before DNA (a discovery made possible by a mind given by God) gave us the ability to identify a human baby as a person made with all the qualities of our maker. The fact that we now know what we do explains in part the age of accountability for right and wrong. It also lets us know that those aborted children have a spiritual identity (name) and go directly to be with Jesus.

The killing of babies obviously breaks the sixth commandment and is a sin like breaking any other commandment is a sin <u>and can be forgiven like all sins.</u> Some women have unfortunately never understood that. God still loves to cleanse all hearts. John 3:16 says, "For God so loved the <u>world</u> that He gave His only begotten Son that whosoever believes in Him should not perish, but have *everlasting <u>life</u>*."

A major part of the claimed need for abortion is the breakup of the family, especially the lack of fathers. According to the Annie Casey Foundation, in the United States today, nearly 24 million children live in a single-parent family. This total, which has been rising for half a century, covers about one in every three kids across America.

Here are a couple of letters, the first from my son to me and the second from me to my son, about thirty years apart. I include this because it seemed to me that too much parenting in our family was left to Norma; also, to hopefully show that the influence of a father in the home is important.

Jeff Lane   5/12/94
Colorado Springs, Colorado

To: Raymond Lane
Larsen Place
Santa Clara, California

This is a long-overdue letter detailing my appreciation for my daddy.

General
    You did a much better than average job at raising me. In fact, I don't know of anyone who has a better dad. You struck a really good balance between discipline and freedom, and gradually gave me more freedom and responsibilities.
    One of the most important lessons I learned from you is a lack of hypocrisy in what you say and do, which is especially hard for a preacher. Thanks for teaching me to be a critical thinker and for teaching me the arts of

conversation and debate. Thanks for encouraging me to enter whatever career I wanted, except maybe football. My attitude about my ability to do whatever I want has descended from your and mom's encouragement and I know this to be an absolutely indispensable attribute for an artist, or any worthwhile person. Thanks for passing on an entrepreneurial outlook on life. Thanks for showing me how to prioritize and what to make important in my life.

Thanks for showing me the value of a dollar and how to spend it and how not to spend it. Thanks for never letting me perceive, as a child, that I was poor or needy (I still don't know whether I was rich or poor!).

Thanks for allowing me to sit and play with bugs for hours. Thanks for encouraging me to build dams in the ditches and houses out of hay bales and piles of firewood.

Thanks for being macho. Really: for helping me understand maleness and what makes a guy a man's man, and at the same time sensitive to others' needs, especially your wife (what a balance).

Thanks for exposing me to great and holy people so that I may contrast them with the majority and so that I may have something to work up to, and for reinforcing the truth that work and holiness are indeed valuable commodities in this world and the next. Thanks for getting me grounded in the Bible and the Church of Jesus Christ. Thanks for stressing the importance and worth of virginity. Thanks for marrying Mom.

Thanks for preaching on using your gifts the same week my high school art teacher encouraged me to enter a career in art. Thanks for listening to the mind of God.

Things we did

Thanks for taking me camping and fishing.

Thanks for forcing me to roof and dig ditches; most people don't know how to do these things well and are amazed when I show them the breadth of my projects.

Thanks for showing me how to handle a tractor, car, typewriter (you forced me to take the class and I got a C), books, chess, Yahtzee, baseball, football, basketball, paintbrush and roller, post hole digger, carpet cleaning, porch railing installation, Canon FTb, hammer, condom (just checking to see if you're awake), saw, drill, grinder, radial arm saw, portable saw, engine overhauling, lawn mower, heifers, oats, mice, powdered milk, milking machines, bulk tanks, shovels, guns, and banty chickens. Thanks for not haranguing me when I was a lazy high school student and lay around in my room all day. It was just a phase. Thanks for understanding how the tires on the 710 wore out after only 12,000 miles, and how the big dent in the bottom of the gas tank was just there. Thanks for not making me take piano lessons. Thanks for not making me eat broccoli.

The great provider

Thanks for my 6-speed Schwinn, and walking with me in downtown Boise to get it and marveling at how they can shoehorn a 427 into those Corvettes. Thanks for the great Christmas presents. I still have a box full of Hot Wheels cards. Thanks for all the model cars. Thanks for letting me blow them up with firecrackers and photographing the destruction.

Thanks for stopping at the park in Boise on a Sunday afternoon to watch the model rockets fly and then allowing me to purchase one a couple of years later.

Thanks for offering to help pay for college. Thanks for emptying your nest into the Dobson and MANC family nest. Thanks for loans. Thanks for what must have been incredible dental bills and orthodontic bills.

Thanks for going to Chicago so you could turn around and get a plane home when I broke my arm and was in traction in the hospital for a week.

Thanks for officiating at my wedding.

Thanks for always peroviding good food. Thanks for Saturday nights at A&W, the Golden Wheel, and Meridian Speedway. Thanks for Sears jeans with double knees and Levi's super slims, cowboy boots and hats, for Converse basketball shoes, and not making me wear ties.

I love you, Dad.

Sincerely,
Jeff

In 2017 I had joined Jeff at the M.D. Anderson complex in Houston, Texas (one of the best cancer treatment facilities in the world), to hear what the verdict was on the treatment he had been receiving for his pancreatic cancer. His medical training as a medical illustrator (MA), and physical condition did not leave much room for an optimistic result to come in the consult after tests the day before. The doctors came in, and in the kindest way possible came to the place of saying, "There is nothing more we can do."

The next day Jeff, my wife, and I rode to the airport in a shuttle; we said our final goodbye outside the terminal. He was going home to his son in Colorado Springs, and Muriel and I to our home in Valley Center, California. We had sat for hours in our hotel room the night before in quiet contemplation thanking God for our lives here and the life to come. John Wesley once said, "Our people die well." Truer words were never spoken than when Jeff's turn was coming.

When the great Christian and scientist Sir Michael Faraday was dying, some journalists questioned him as to his speculations for a life after death. "SPECULATIONS ... I know nothing about speculations. I'm resting on certainties! I know that my redeemer lives, and because he lives, I shall live also!"

The following letter was written and mailed four days after we had said goodbye ... things were a little blurry at the time, but I believe the letter was received shortly before he literally saw the angels coming for him.

May 16, 2017

Jeff,

Last week I told you that the most precious possession that I have in my safe is a letter you wrote to me on Father's Day a few years ago. That's not quite true. *You* are my most precious "possession." Muriel,, Leah and Nate will share that lofty position then, but this misslle is for you. (A little rocketry there.) At some later date I'll be writing a couple of items to them.

In all my years as a pastor, I frequently found myself trying to help parents who had sons that were breaking their hearts in small and large ways. I couldn't help them a whole lot because I had never walked in their shoes. You <u>never</u> caused your parents deep pain in the heart. On rare occasions you might have caused a little concern about some choices, but you always chose to do the right thing. I can't help but wonder what part all the scripture memorized in *Caravans* (children's program) might have been hidden in some crevice in your brain and affected your life, without your conscious awareness, to do the right thing.

Sometimes when parents get together they lapse into a "my kid is better that your kid" time. I'm guilty of getting into that conversation on a few occasions because I knew that my son was the best.

You seemed to be gifted by God to be generous with your time, money, and talent. You have performed in awesome ways as a father, teacher, mentor, and husband. Being a husband can be an almost overwhelming challenge at times (from a three-time winner [now four]). Melinda (who died of pancreatic cancer fifteen months before) had her own approach to life, and you helped her to be an achiever in her life's work. (She was an executive editor and ordained in the Episcopal Church.) Your love and protection there was obvious and sometimes amazing to her in-laws.

When the history of what has resulted from your teaching is known a generation from now, it would seem certain that your efforts will be richly rewarded by the achievements of those who have had the privilege of calling you teacher in all the classroom and rocketry experiences.

Your patience is so far above what I have ever achieved, I can't even comprehend it. Frequently throughout the years, friends have said to me, "Be patient." And my thought is, *I want patience and I want it now.*

Then, there is creativity in your artwork. To have

the "Best of Show" at the state fair was great. Hopefully, that particular item will receive the acclaim it deserves someday. Your book work in creating covers and doing layouts has been that of a winner.

When you were complimented by Dad about your carpentry skills, you said you learned the basics from him. I could never do "finish" work like you did. What you did to that old house is simply awesome! You would like to have completed the job, but I doubt that it is possible for some jobs to ever be "finished."

What an amazing mechanic. Who would have thought that tearing apart and reassembling a Datsun would have led to knowing how to fix cars from end to end. You saved a fortune there.

Oh—mischievousness. Even last week on the darkest of days of this life, there were glimpses of quirkiness. Wonderful ... amazing.

Parent: Nate inherited great genes and you and Melinda have enabled him to face life through more traumas, grief, and heartache than anyone his age should have to face. Making tough decisions and acting in a good way has laid the foundation that will serve him well in the future. While we wish he didn't have the challenges he has, we can be confident that he will perform satisfactorily.

It's pretty special that God has already said that He has prepared a place for you. Actually, we are told that our prayers, obedience, and love play a part in the building materials for our eternal home. So your place will be pretty nice. There are at least a couple people "keeping the light on" for you. Your mom let me know from heaven that it is indescribably wonderful and you will feel that way for eternity too.

Well, may God's grace sustain your journey, from the man who loves you as much as a man can in his frailness and by His help,

Dad.

CONCLUSION

There is an old question that is told in church circles that goes like this: "What does it mean when a pastor says 'in conclusion?'" ... "It doesn't mean a darn thing because the pastor is likely to make another point."

Yes, but I just want to say that it is my hope and prayer that people around the world will "come to their senses" rather than have a few minutes of emotion, and value life by taking responsibility for their sexual activity.

P.S. Doesn't it seem strange to have a month of celebration each June to celebrate individuals that either can't or don't want to have a baby? I just feel bad for them.

ADDENDUM

This book shares some of the experiences and actions of my life, but it includes very little of my thinking. My mentor, Al Jones, says my brain never sleeps. That is somewhat true, and it's usually a compliment.

In the early part of *CONCEIVED*, there were small snippets of truth about when we become human beings. There are some mighty implications that need to be considered, so here goes.

In John 10:10 in the NIV Bible, Jesus says: "The thief comes only to steal and kill and destroy; I have come that they may have life, and have it to the full." Most of the life shared in this book has to a significant degree been the kind of existence Jesus says life for a person created in the image of God should be like … the life Jesus modeled for us during his earthly years … a life full of love, joy, peace, kindness, goodness, faithfulness, gentleness, and self-control as stated in Galatians 5:22–23. Productivity, messenger, servant, teacher, persecuted, and much more could also be added to personhood.

When I was preaching, the thief part of John 10:10 didn't get enough coverage. I'm afraid much of the world experiences massive doses of the "thief" … Satan or man thinking he (or she) is God. Can you just think for a moment what effect

ADDENDUM

stealing can have on a life, or the loss of the life of a pet or family member, or a possession destroyed? Are you thinking?

So, where is this going? To the death of babies, of course. In Israel last week, some terrorists did a lot of stealing, killing, and destroying. Do you know how many wars start because someone says, "We are justified in doing this"? Virtually all. Today someone you never knew can say, "you dissed or hurt my feelings," and attack you orally or with a weapon.

Let's try to touch on just one aspect. There was an eruption of emotion over the babies killed, okay? Do you suppose God might see this as very similar to when an abortionist removes a baby piece by piece from a mother? Are you thinking?

Is it murder to deliberately take another person's life? The sixth commandment says it is. Is it a sin? In I John 3, we read that anyone who breaks the law (sixth commandment in this case) is a sinner. Hold on now, this does have a direction: can a sinner be forgiven even of the most grievous sins? The answer is "yes of course." In the Old Testament King David committed adultery and murder, yet he repented in Psalm 51, and the Bible says later that David was "a man after God's own heart" (Acts 13:22 & 23).

The New Testament is full of letting us know that our repentance leads to God's forgiveness. See Acts 3:19 for instance.

Does this have you thinking about the sacrifices of infants by the ancients to their gods, by abortions throughout the history of man, by the killer of a baby, jealous of the attention of its mother? Can one be totally disconnected from the other? Our Creator God is the same yesterday and forever.

Jesus said in Matthew 19:12–14 KJV, "Let the little children come to me, and do not hinder them, for the kingdom of heaven belongs to such as these." This has major implications.

Have you heard of nature or nurture as to how and when

the spiritual condition of an individual is developed? Basically, nature is believing a person's spiritual condition is established by going back to conception as we now know it. Nurture is the education, training, and teaching that a child gets. This is where the "age of accountability" comes in.

What is the situation of the person that tells a child early on that his job in life is to kill the person on the other side of the fence when you get the opportunity? Are we having fun yet? I'm not trying to get to the extreme bottom of this issue—it would take a library.

To stimulate some thinking, consider the Bible story of the Samaritan woman (hated by the Jews) at the well. Jesus considered her valuable and she became a believer in Him. "…Jesus loves the little children of the world, red and yellow, black and white, Jesus loves the little children of the world," the song rightly says.

So what? Well, it means that the babies that were slaughtered whether in abortion or some other way had their spirits go immediately to be with Jesus. I doubt the perpetrators would be happy to know that. Think about it.

If you remember earlier in *CONCEIVED*, there were references to my belief that my siblings may have missed one life, but they certainly have eternal life with God.

Do you need more to think about?

Maybe yes, maybe no, but thanks so much for getting involved with me.

ADDENDUM II

Science says that human life begins in the womb. That's WHERE it begins. But WHEN is the exact moment it begins? Do we know the answer to that question?

Unequivocally … YES. We know.

Science has answered that question for us too. According to a 1996 Princeton study, "development of the embryo begins at stage one, when a sperm fertilizes an oocyte and together they form a zygote." A zygote is the scientific term for a fertilized egg.

In plain English, at the moment of conception, when the egg is fertilized, **a new human life is formed**, complete with its own genetically unique DNA. Unique DNA means it is actually a new human person, not a genetic copycat of its parent.

Dr. Jerome Lejeune, a French pediatrician and geneticist, is perhaps best known for discovering the extra chromosome responsible for Down syndrome. However, his research also proved that the **full human genetic code** is present in the human embryo from the moment of sperm-egg fusion. That means that this "zygote" actually is a unique, distinct, and individual person—with its own fingerprint! This genetic code is not just any genetic code. It is an **unrepeatable**, human genetic code—completely different from the mother and father.

In his book "Life is a Blessing," Dr. Lejeune wrote, "*To accept the fact that, after fertilization has taken place, a new human has come into being, is no longer a matter of taste or of opinion. The human nature of the human being from conception to old age is not a metaphysical contention. It is plain, experimental evidence.*"

Essentially, **when** life begins is not up for debate anymore. A unique human person exists immediately at the moment of conception.

It seems unfathomable to me that in the twenty-first century with all the current science (man's discovery of God's activity), we can still think it is okay to kill another person.

ENDORSEMENTS

I have known Ray Lane for some time now and I find his biblical knowledge and way of relaying it to his students and to his friends as being kind, sensitive, and knowledgeable in every respect.

No one portrays, in both word and deed, the essence of Biblical Truth better than does Ray. His words written here, and his life lived, represent the foundation of a meaningful faith that is, at once, both functional, adaptable, and sustainable under every circumstance he encounters in day-to-day life.

Read what he has to say carefully and prayerfully. You will be inspired.

—Dr. Robert D. Strand, Veterinarian

Luke 17:21: "Neither shall they say Lo Here! Or Lo There! For behold the Kingdom of GOD is within you!" Christ said it, and this describes you.

—Calvin Johnson, Retired USAF Navigator

You are a wonderful man we had the blessed opportunity to know personally and would be honored to endorse you as an author or writer! Thank you for all the help you have given my children in the past.

Gratefully,
Leisa R. Dwyer, Church member

My thoughts on Mr. Lane:

On our life journeys we meet many people, some who leave a hole in our hearts and others who leave our hearts more whole. I had the pleasure of meeting Ray after his whirlwind courtship and then marriage to my mother in the summer of 2014. He was the answer to her years of praying for a man of God. We formed a connection quickly with our common interest of cattle and agriculture. Always easy to talk to and good for a laugh or two.

We are all part of the light of God; some of us shine a little while and some shine big. To think that Ray might not have ever been able to shine his light is inconceivable to me. Ray's light has touched so many souls for the better.

His conversations always warm my heart and leave it more whole.

Kathy Kroeker, daughter of Ray Lane since 2014

It is easy for me to recommend Ray's book to others. During the 1970s, when I was in high school, I took oil painting lessons from Norma for three years. Due to Ray and Norma's influence, I developed a lifelong love of painting. More importantly, I received a witness of two lives devoted to Jesus Christ. I am more grateful for sharing their love of God with me than for the art lessons. My husband, son, daughter, and I are all followers of the Lord too. I pray that Ray's book will show God's love to many more people.

    Denise Chalfon—Artist

If part of understanding faith is that it's an action based on belief, my longtime friend of many years, Ray Lane, embodies that truth. He is a man of strong faith. This book is an outcome of his beliefs and consequent action.

    —Rev. Al Jones, Pastor-Missionary

I have known Ray Lane for about three years. He is a retired minister, a good friend, and the kind of person that I am quite comfortable with and trust him in every way.

    —Betty Hall, Student and Teacher

I met Ray Lane a few years ago, late in both of our lives, and regret I had not met him sooner. Ray is a good-natured, caring individual with a sincere interest in anyone he meets. A casual acquaintance quickly became a very good friend. Ray is someone you want to be with if looking for help with unpacking a complex issue you're dealing with. His principled life experiences, from being a very successful farmer to a sought-after pastor, contribute to his acceptance as a powerful and personal life mentor.

    —Dick Daleke, Retired Navy Officer

ACKNOWLEDGEMENTS

Wife #1
Norma Jean Lane, partner in all things.
Introduced me to the Lord.
Artist extraordinaire, outstanding Bible
preacher. Went to heaven because
of heart failure on her 76th birthday in
the 57th year of our marriage.

Wife #2
Ramona Jean Lane, an intense searcher
of all things spiritual. An
example of "Blessed are those who hunger and thirst after
righteousness" (Matthew 5:6). Died of COPD.

Wife #3
Muriel Hope Lane, forever a soldier
in the Salvation Army, now
ringing bells on streets of gold. Surprised us with pancreatic
cancer and departed in three weeks.

Wife #4
Joyce Ann Johnson Lane, shares in listening to outstanding
ministers. Retired nurse always ready to help me or anyone
else in whatever way is needed. We race through the 90,s
together, hand in hand, heart joined in heart.

SUPPORTING FRIENDS AND FAMILY

Grandson Nathaniel Patrick Lane
Daughter Leah & Husband Lee Smit
Dr. Alfred & Kitty Jones
Bernice & Sons Art & Calvin Johnson
Floranne Young
Rev. Dennis & Gwen Norman
Betty Hall
USMC Rev. Colonel Tyler & Cathy Ryberg
Bob & Verna Glanville
USN Capt. Dick & Ellen Dalke
Vicki Nofsinger
Ralph & Jimmie Bohannon
Arlene Pellegrino
Duane & Esther Harder
Emeline Holz

Chuck & Audrey Melby
Bob & Janet Hayton
Ira & Janet Kobre
Ward Adams
Cliff Butler
Raoul & Bridgitte Gott
Jan & Lou Scholl
Dr. Dick & Jan Ferguson
Dr. David & Denny Greb
Chuck & Pam Grabill
Buryl & Sandi Mellema
Cleve Beckwith
Dan Flowers
Stan Katsura
Randy & Linda Haskel

Pastor Ray
3377 Mill Vista Rd. #3409,
Highlands Ranch, CO 80129

Printed in the USA
CPSIA information can be obtained
at www.ICGtesting.com
CBHW071321030224
3985CB00007B/22